THINKING ABOUT PLAYS
A GUIDE FOR DRAMA AND SPEECH STUDENTS

KEN PICKERING
AND
GILES AUCKLAND-LEWIS

EDITED BY

JOHN NICHOLAS

Dramatic Lines*

DRAMATIC LINES, TWICKENHAM, ENGLAND
Thinking About Plays
text copyright © Ken Pickering and Giles Auckland-Lewis
2004

Dramatic Lines
PO Box 201
Twickenham
TW2 5RQ
England

A CIP record for this book is
available from the British Library

ISBN 1 904557 14 7

Thinking About Plays
first published in 2004
by
Dramatic Lines
Twickenham England

Printed by The Dramatic Lines Press
Twickenham England

FOREWORD

This **THINKING ABOUT PLAYS Handbook** is one of a series primarily designed to support students and teachers preparing for examinations from the Drama and Speech syllabus of Trinity College, *London.*

However, the Dramatic Lines Handbooks have much wider applications. Not only do they provide accessible and practical advice to students working towards ANY examination in Drama, Speech, Communication or Performing Arts, they also give invaluable help to those who wish to use their skills in a professional capacity as performers, teachers or communicators.

The Handbooks are quite literally something to keep to hand whenever you are working towards an important examination, performance, audition or presentation and you will find that they become your constant companions for a life in the Performance and Communications Arts.

Ken Pickering

Ken Pickering

Chief Examiner for Drama and Speech at
Trinity College, *London* and Professor of Arts Education
at the Institute for Arts in Therapy and Education

CONTENTS

To Nigel Mintram 1964 – 2002

Teacher ✳ Actor ✳ Friend

INTRODUCTION

Whether you are studying drama, involved in the production of plays, writing about or watching them . . . . . you need to think about plays.

Whenever you take an examination in speech and drama, acting or some other aspect of theatre, you will almost certainly be asked questions about plays - and it is probable that it will be those that you have presented as part of your work.

These questions provide an opportunity for you to show that you have been thinking as you prepare to perform or write about some aspect of a play.

thinking to use your mind for arriving at conclusions; to have an opinion, to consider, to judge.

Actors, directors, designers, students and even audiences, have to make hundreds of decisions about the way in which they approach a play and these all require careful thought. The outcomes may be very different, but the process of thinking may need to be very similar.

This handbook does not tell you <u>what</u> to think but we do make many suggestions as to <u>how</u> you might think about plays.

You may argue that all this emphasis on thinking will take the enjoyment out of theatre. In fact, precisely the opposite is true! There is probably nothing more enjoyable about a play than thinking about it, whether we are directing a production, performing it, watching it or writing about it.

Performers, students and critics all need to think . . . . but where do they start?

Ken Pickering and Giles Auckland-Lewis

1   HOW TO USE THIS BOOK

You must have guessed that we are going to ask you to do a lot of thinking. DON'T try to read the whole book through quickly; take each section and read it several times, pause and think about it and, if possible, discuss it.

We have included a number of quotations from playwrights, directors and critics in the book and ask you to ⇨ THINK ABOUT THESE. The quotations may be a direct challenge to something we have said or may stimulate you to think in another way. In addition to thinking about these, try to think of examples from your own experience that will fit some of the ideas we have raised.

There are a great many facts in the book but they are NOT there to be <u>remembered</u>. The facts are there to help you <u>understand</u> but DON'T worry if you forget any of them. However, the more you understand, the more you will remember, and this will enable you to use the information we give you more fully.

Most important of all, keep on testing out what we have said against your own experience. For example, if you are preparing to present a scene or speech from a play as part of an examination, audition or festival, refer to any topics that you consider appropriate, think about the information and use the ideas we have suggested as you read the entire play. You will be surprised at the difference in your approach and the improvement in your work.

➡ THINK ABOUT THIS

We need writers to help us describe our lives and to make sense of them.

Richard Eyre, 2000

2 PLAYS

Most people begin their study of drama and theatre by reading, watching or taking part in plays. A play will probably be the work of a single writer but it may be the result of collaboration between several writers or even devised by a group through improvisation. Whatever the process involved, a play has to be shaped from various elements, which is why we describe someone who creates plays as a **playwright**.

moves it
Magicians
every
The Fool

playwright *a person who writes plays; a dramatist*

Every year, thousands of new plays are written in the English language, alone. For example, the Actors' Theatre of Louisville in the USA received 700 entries for their recent playwriting competition. Yet, of the thousands of plays written, few will be performed and even fewer will go on to be published or performed again. It does seem, however, that there is something about the human condition that makes us want to explore it continually through drama.

Iroborus
instantly
Creates
Drama

In television and film, particularly, we now tend to discriminate between endeavours to make a serious investigation of life – which we label 'drama'; and the obvious attempts at 'entertaining' – which we might label 'comedy' or 'thriller'. Most playwrights would maintain that this is all **drama** and that when this is

The Fool

transferred to the stage it is **theatre**.

drama   *a story, told by means of dialogue and action, to be performed by actors*

theatre   *the writing and production of plays*

➡️ THINK ABOUT THESE

> Theatre consists of this: in making live representations of reported or invented happenings between human beings, and doing so with a view to entertainment. At any rate that is what we shall mean when we speak of theatre, whether old or new.
>
> Bertold Brecht, 1948

> The great dramatist has something better to do than to amuse himself or his audience. He has to interpret life.
>
> George Bernard Shaw, 1909

The motives for writing a play may range from passionate political, religious or social commitment, to a desire to entertain, disturb or influence an audience. In more practical terms, a play may result from a commission to write something for a specific number

4

of performers on a particular topic or simply from the need to keep a theatre company solvent.

Alan Ayckbourn, one of Britain's most successful contemporary playwrights, was disarmingly honest about this when he said in an interview that unless he wrote a new play each year for his Scarborough theatre, it would cease to function.

In total contrast, another of Britain's most influential modern playwrights, Harold Pinter, told a meeting of students:

> 'What I write has no obligation to anything other than to itself. My responsibility is not to audiences, critics, producers, directors, and actors or to my fellow men in general, but to the play in hand, simply . . . . . I have usually begun a play in quite a simple manner; found a couple of characters in a particular context, thrown them together and listened to what they said . . . . . '

Both playwrights are, no doubt, equally anxious to have their plays performed and, although their work is very different, they have both made statements resisting the idea that their plays should 'instruct' or contain a 'message' for their audience.

➡ TRY THIS

You might like to compare Ayckbourn and Pinter's approach to writing with that of the 20th century German playwright and director, Bertold Brecht, who described a number of his plays as 'Lehrstucke' – that is 'teaching pieces'.

➡ THINK ABOUT THIS

I'm on a crusade to try to persuade people that theatre can be fun; but every time I start doing that, some hairy . . . . . from the left comes in and tells them it's instructive and drives them all out again. If I want to be instructed, I go to night school. I may be instructed in the theatre, but I don't go there predominantly for instruction: I go to the theatre for entertainment.

Alan Ayckbourn, 1981

The process of writing a play can be just as varied as the motive. Whereas, for example, Pinter refuses to explain his characters or his way of working in any detail, the great 19th century Norwegian playwright, Henrik Ibsen left copious notes of his intentions for his plays and characters.

Discussing his play *Ghosts*, he wrote:

> '. . . . . this play is to be like a picture of life . . . . .
> they are to be happy, but this is only so in
> appearance . . . . . everything is ghosts . . . . .
> these modern women, ill-used as daughters, as
> sisters, as wives, not educated according to their
> gifts, prevented from following their calling,
> deprived of their inheritance, embittered in
> temper – it is these who furnish the mothers of
> the new generation. What will be the result?'

Whatever the process involved in the creation of a play, we almost invariably end up with a **play text** or **play script** as the basis for performance.

play text   *the actual structure of words in a written play*

play script   *the manuscript, or a copy of the play text*

We have surviving play texts from 2,500 years of European and English-speaking theatre, alone. Some of these will have become established classics, others will remain comparatively obscure and, as we have already seen, the number is being added to daily.

So we shall begin with a question . . . . .

Q   What can we expect to find in a play text?

3   INFORMATION

This may seem a rather surprising element to place first, but, in fact, play texts do contain a great deal of information about characters, environments and situations.

⇨ TRY THIS

Read a page or two of a play and then make a checklist of what you have learned already about: CHARACTERS * ENVIRONMENTS * SITUATIONS

NOTE: You need to be aware that a playwright may deliberately make it difficult for us to make <u>sense</u> of information sometimes - but that is often true of 'real life'.

4 DIALOGUE

This usually takes the form of talk between characters but it may also contain some 'inner' dialogue in which a character appears to be talking to, or with, himself / herself in a **soliloquy**.

soliloquy   *lines in which a character reveals his / her thoughts to the audience but not to other characters by speaking as if to himself / herself*

A play text may take the form of a **monologue** in which a character speaks alone and addresses the audience directly. The English playwright David Hare's play *Via Dolorosa,* for example, consists entirely of a monologue performed by the playwright.

monologue   *a play or part of a play for one actor only*

Dialogue may simulate everyday speech or it may be in verse, as it is in the plays of William Shakespeare or T S Eliot. Alternatively, dialogue may approximate speech by means of a stream of atonal ritualistic utterances or it may provide a disjointed and apparently meaningless sound.

However, regardless of the type or style dialogue may take, we often look to it to provide distinctive voices for the characters and insights into their thoughts and motives.

➡️ THINK ABOUT THESE

Modern playwrights begin their plays with angels, scoundrels and clowns exclusively.

Anton Chekhov, 1887

The theatre, as conceived of in the period between the two World Wars, and as it is perhaps still thought of in the United States today, is a theatre of characters. The analysis of characters and their confrontation was the theatre's chief concern.

Jean Paul Sartre, 1946

5   CHARACTERS

One of the most extraordinary and fascinating aspects of theatre is the process whereby an actor takes the playwright's words from the printed page and turns them into a **character**.

Words
Grown up
essence
Qualities
+
rehertypes
+
herarchship

character   *the essential quality, attributes and characteristics of a person portrayed by an actor or actress*

Many playwrights would claim that it is they who have created the characters and this view would seem to be supported by the tendency for students and critics, without themselves having been involved in acting, to write about characters as if they were real people.

The 20th century American playwright Tennessee Williams's strength lay in creating and manipulating interesting characters caught up in critical or violent situations as they seek to recover a past or create a future more satisfying than the vulgar and materialistic present. Then, as the dramatic action progresses, the protagonist is forced to abandon his / her illusions, after physical or moral degradation at the hands of callous or vicious characters as Williams focuses on the inner truth of character and situation. Blanche in *A Streetcar Named Desire* is a character such as this.

When he was describing how he came to write the

short play *That Kind of Couple*, the young contemporary American playwright Shawn Telford said:

> '. . . . . what happened subsequently was a dialogue that began in my head and got progressively louder until I had to write it to get those two characters to shut the hell up!'

On the other hand, we shall find that some of the best minds in the modern theatre have been focused on the actors themselves 'creating' characters.

Generally, we seem to expect characters to speak and act as recognizable human beings – but this breaks down when we find that the dialogue of the play hardly resembles everyday speech.

To complicate matters even further, playwrights differ considerably in what they tell us directly about their characters.

Dublin born, George Bernard Shaw and the 20th century American playwright Arthur Miller, for instance, give extensive notes on the appearance and background of their characters in the text, whereas Christopher Marlowe, Shakespeare and Pinter give us no such information.

In some plays, such as the medieval *Everyman,* the characters appear to be the embodiment of an idea rather than 'real' people, and in the plays *Not I* and *Krapp's Last Tape* by Samuel Beckett we have characters that are no more than a mouth or a tape recorder!

6   ACTION

We are not only concerned with what characters say but also with what they do.

Playwrights often give us clues to this in the dialogue: Shakespeare, for example, often uses lines like 'look where she comes!' to indicate the entrance of a character.

Sometimes we have very specific stage directions. Ibsen, for instance, gives precise instructions in his text as to where and when he wants his characters to move, and these movements are closely allied to the situations and attitudes of the characters.

A number of plays are dense with stage directions giving elaborate details of the setting and what is happening on stage. For example, in his play *Ghost Sonata* the great Swedish dramatist, August Strindberg, sets up a complete scenario on stage before anyone actually speaks.

Action and activity

Theatre directors and critics have sometimes discriminated between **action** and **activity**.

action   describes the sequence of happenings, the broad sweep of what is actually happening in a play activity   *any specific action or pursuit, covering all the trivial things which people do, like standing, laughing or lighting a cigarette*

NOTE: Actors often find activities helpful in finding and understanding their characters. In Kevin Elyot's drama about gay manners and morals, *My Night With Reg*, for example, the fashion in which Guy permanently busies himself around the flat and fusses over his guests gives a terrific insight into his character.

⇨ THINK ABOUT THIS

I can sum up none of my plays. I can describe none of them, except to say: That is what happened. That is what they said. That is what they did.

Harold Pinter, 1970

Whatever actions are carried out on stage, we expect the text to provide a reason for them.

Such reasons are usually described as **motivation** and form the basis of many approaches to the understanding of character. Even if an action is irrational or inexplicable we still need to know <u>why</u> this is the case.

motivation   some inner drive, impulse or intention that causes a person to do something or act in a certain way

Often, an act will derive from the tensions that exist between characters or from the tensions within a character and these may or may not be revealed in the dialogue.

The more we search for a character's motivation, the more we need to understand the whole context in which the character is operating. So exploration of the detail of the play includes careful observation of human behaviour and research into a range of social and historical factors that may influence the fictional characters.

➡ THINK ABOUT THESE

Observation is a major part of acting.

Bertold Brecht, 1948

I really believe, that for very profound reasons, there's a close link between drama and politics. There are deeper reasons for that than the obvious fact that politicians must be skilled in media showmanship and act on camera. That's just an external similarity. What is drama? It's an attempt at a concisely structured expression of time events. . . . . . of life. And politics too, is a densely structured version of life.

Václav Havel

playwright and President of the Czech Republic, 1993 -1999

The **subtext** of a play usually remains unspoken or, as in real life a character may say exactly the opposite to what he or she actually means.

subtext   is what lies beneath the surface of what is said in a play

Moving from the text itself to the subtext is the job of the actor and director in rehearsal or in the case of an examination candidate, in the preparation. The thoughts which produce the words must be imagined so that it appears in performance as if the characters are thinking those thoughts and speaking those words for the first time.

As the great contemporary Polish director, Tadeus Bradewcki (b.1945) puts it:

'. . . it must be born afresh in you each evening!'

The use of words

We can use words in many ways:

* to express ourselves honestly

* to deceive

- to comfort

- to give information

- to flatter

- to provoke

- to persuade

- to influence

- to intimidate

. . . . . and so on.

When we study a play text we must explore why certain words are used and what motivates the characters that use them.

Theatre is one of the oldest forms of storytelling and we should be able to discern the storyline or **plot** of a play from the text.

plot   the plan of action of a play

The plot may be carefully crafted with strategically placed tensions, climaxes, and a final moment when everything seems to come to a head, which we call a **denouement**.

denouement   the outcome, solution, unravelling or clarification of a plot

If all of this takes the form of a three or four act play, we may well label it 'a well-made play'. On the other hand, a text may be almost surrealist, with actions and words that appear to make little logical sense; or else our expectations are cheated because what we might expect to happen does not happen.

Subplot

The main plot of a play normally concerns the major characters but there may be one or more **subplots** built around secondary characters.

subplot   a secondary or subordinate plot in a play

A satisfying way of approaching a text is to realize that every character has a story and it is the interweaving of these stories and the juxtaposition of the plot with the various subplots that gives a play so much of its interest. Look at Shakespeare's scene with Bottom and the other mechanicals rehearsing a play within the play *A Midsummer Night's Dream* for a wonderful example of a subplot.

⇨ THINK ABOUT THIS

The Theatre has to tell us stories about ourselves: then we listen to them.

Richard Eyre, 2001

Plays have been printed in the English language since the early 16th century, although, for a long period after that, many survived in hand-written form only. It is therefore important when looking at recent editions of old plays to remember that subsequent editors may have changed some of the original.

One way in which 16th and 17th century play texts differ from more recent plays is in the use of the word **scene.**

scene   a part of a play that constitutes a unit of development or action as a passage between characters; a division of a play, usually part of an act, in which conventionally the action is continuous and in a single place.

In early play texts a new scene began every time a new character was introduced, whereas, in more recent years we have tended to think of a scene as a change of location.

Look at the plays of the English playwright Ben Jonson for interesting examples of early play texts. One of his first plays *Every Man in His Humour,* was performed in 1598 with Shakespeare in the cast!

STRUCTURE

From the printed text we can see the **structure** that the playwright has given to the play.

structure   *manner of building, constructing and organising of the work*

Play structures include:

> **plays with acts and scenes** - as in the work of Ibsen, such as *A Doll's House*.

> **plays in episodes** - as in the work of Brecht, such as *Mother Courage and her Children*.

> **plays in two halves with an interlude** - as in T S Eliot's *Murder in the Cathedral*.

> **plays with continuous action** – as in Thornton Wilder's *The Skin of Our Teeth*.

> **plays punctuated by songs** – as in *Oklahoma!* The musical play by librettist / lyricist Oscar Hammerstein II based on the play *Green Grow the Lilacs* by Lynn Riggs.

All these possible structures have very practical applications because they provide the director and actors with units for rehearsal, staging and inner rhythm.

FORM

In addition to looking at the structure of a play, the **form** that a play takes also needs to be taken into consideration.

form   the way in which the parts of the whole are organised; style

We can see the **form** that the playwright has chosen as well as the structure, by looking at the play text.

The form that a play takes includes:

➤ **the full-length play** – with a running time of several hours to constitute an entire evening at the theatre such as William Shakespeare's *Henry V.*

➤ **the one-act or short play** – possibly no longer than ten minutes or even a piece lasting thirty seconds, Samuel Beckett's *Breath*!

The choices are by no means arbitrary and the form invariably relates to the content and intention of the play.

➡ THINK ABOUT THESE

I have been thinking a good deal about plays lately and I have been wondering why I dislike the clear and logical construction which seems necessary if one is to succeed on the Modern Stage.

W B Yeats, 1913

For me, a creator of theatre, the important thing is not the words but what we do with these words, what gives life to the inanimate words of the text, what transforms them into 'the Word'.

Jerzy Grotowski, 1968

The play text, consisting largely but not exclusively of the words spoken by the characters, is not simply a series of 'sound bites' – although inexperienced playwrights often make this mistake. Even the 'top' text of a play will have layers of meaning for the actors, director and audience to discover.

Words may have **literal**, **ironic** or **allegorical** meaning.

literal   representing the exact ordinary meaning; not figurative or symbolical

ironic   the contrary of what is expressed; directly opposite of what is or might be expected

allegorical   the description of one thing under the image of another; people, things and happenings with hidden or symbolic meanings

For example in J B Priestley's popular play *An Inspector Calls* we may choose to interpret the character of the Inspector as an embodiment of the consciences of the other characters, existing only in their imaginations.

It is speculation like this which makes the study of drama so fascinating and ensures that plays have what actor and director Dr Jonathan Miller (b.1934), described as 'an afterlife' long after they have been written.

In order to achieve such understanding we need to allow ourselves plenty of time for thought and rumination and not expect a text to yield up all its levels at a first or even a second reading. This of course, runs contrary to our current passion for instant communication and neatly packaged statements and answers to questions.

Non-verbal information

Although a play text consists largely of words spoken (or sung) by the characters, the playwright also provides us with relevant non-verbal information.

Non-verbal codes of communication and sign systems include:

- lighting

- sets

- properties

- costumes

- actions

- dances

- music

- sound

- special effects

Let us take lighting as an example. Lighting is one of the non-verbal codes of communication and sign systems for which the text must, to a considerable extent, serve as a blueprint.

Since the development of sophisticated lighting technology in the theatres of the late 19th century, play texts have often included elaborate requirements for colour, intensity, direction and quality of light; and the importance of lighting design and the art of lighting designers is now recognised.

Lighting may convey a time of day, the direction of sunrise or create a specific mood or illusion. Then, as we read the text, we are able to visualise the action, setting and atmosphere of the play and even discuss its symbolism.

lighting *the stage lights collectively; the art, practice, or manner of using and arranging lights on a stage*

The hugely successful West End stage play *The Woman in Black,* for example, adapted for the stage by Stephen Mallatratt from the novel by Susan Hill, is an atmospheric and powerful ghost story that relies heavily on Kevin Sleep's lighting design. Lighting represents a vital element of this production with its cast of two and little by way of set and costume.

NOTE: You should NOT lose sight of the fact that lighting is only one of the non-verbal codes of communication and sign systems that we use in a theatre performance.

 TO FIND OUT MORE: you should refer to the **Non-verbal communication** topic (see 18 CRITICAL THINKING ABOUT PLAYS p.120).

⇨ ASK YOURSELF THESE QUESTIONS:

Q   Can the theatre exist without lighting effects?

Q   Can the theatre exist without costumes and sets?

Q   Can the theatre exist without music to accompany
the plot?

Q   Can the theatre exist without a text?

Q   Can the theatre exist without actors?

Q   Can the theatre exist without an audience?

⇨ THINK ABOUT THIS

> Can the theatre exist without costumes and sets?
> Yes, it can. Can it exist without music to accompany
> the plot? Yes. Can it exist without lighting effects?
> Of course. And without a text? Yes, the history of the
> theatre confirms this. In the evolution of the theatrical
> art, the text was one of the last Elements to be added.
> If we place some people on a stage with a scenario
> they themselves have put together and let them
> improvise their parts as in the Commedia dell 'Arte,
> the performance will be equally good even if the
> words are not articulated but simply muttered. But
> can the theatre exist without actors? I know of no
> example of this . . . . . Can the theatre exist without
> an audience? At least one spectator is needed to
> make it a performance.
>
> Jerzy Grotowski, 1964

The statement you have just read by the remarkable
and influential director and theorist, Jerzy Grotowski
(b.1933), reminds us that we must consider drama
that has no text.

Improvisation, in which the actors invent the plot and
dialogue during rehearsal, is a very rich theatrical

tradition and, in our own time, has produced some of the most famous duos in comedy, such as Eric Morecambe (1926 – 1984) and Ernie Wise (b.1925), for example.

improvisation to compose, or simultaneously compose and perform on the spur of the moment without any preparation

So far as we can tell, there has always been an aspect of performance that relies upon improvisation at every stage of development of the theatre throughout the world.

This form of theatre is currently very popular in colleges, where improvisational comedy is seen as a sport, but we can also find non-scripted drama in street theatre, comedy clubs or revue bars.

More substantial plays devised through improvisation may be used to explore local, social issues; as in the work of Ann Jellicoe in rural Britain, or may take the form of group therapy or 'forum theatre' developed by Augusto Boal (b.1931) the Brazilian theatre director, playwright and theorist, in South America.

There are also many examples of drama which are not derived from one single script but which have drawn upon various written and oral sources such as diaries, interviews, letters, songs, poems and newspaper articles. Plays of this genre frequently take the form of 'one man' or 'one woman' shows, such as *The Hollow Crown* and *Female Parts*.

There are also a substantial number of plays that begin life without a script before reaching a more permanent written stage. This is true of plays such as *Abigail's Party* and *Nuts in May*, the television plays written by British theatre practitioner, Mike Leigh.

Leigh's distinctive work invariably begins with intensive improvisation sessions around given themes in which the actors develop both the characters and the plot. He argues that there is little point in writing plays and then beginning to search for someone to act them; he would far rather build the play around the actors themselves.

NOTE: It is interesting that Leigh's most successful work for the theatre has had a second life on film with *Bleak Moments* and the later films *Life is Sweet, Naked* and *Secrets and Lies,* as well as on television.

➡ THINK ABOUT THESE

Once in our past, in Greek tragedies and comedies, a priest presided over the presentation of drama, indicating that going to the theatre was a matter of life and death. Today, we place theatre and the other arts in the category of entertainment.

Thomas Moore, 1992

Any dramatic form is an artifice, a way of transforming a subjective feeling into something that can be comprehended through public symbols.

Arthur Miller, 1958

Now that we have thought about what a student, actor or director might derive from reading a play text we need to consider the types of play you might come across.

I   REALISM

Realism is the dominant mode of modern drama. We almost always expect our characters to speak as 'real' people and to inhabit a 'real' environment. Indeed, it is difficult for us to imagine that there were substantial periods of theatre history in which realism, as we now understand it, was considered neither important nor appropriate.

realism   the picturing of people and things as it is thought they really are, without idealizing

19th Century Realism

A very significant event in the development of realism was when the playwright, Henrik Ibsen, turned his back on the **Romantic Movement** and stopped writing romantic verse dramas in favour of:

'the very much more difficult art of writing the genuine plain language spoken in real life'

from a letter dated 1883

Romantic Movement   the revolt in the 18th and early 19th century against principles that had become associated with the 17th century neoclassical revival of classic style and form; characterized by freedom of form and spirit, emphasis on feeling and originality, on the personality of the artist himself

Ibsen's plays were introduced into the English-speaking theatre by the playwright George Bernard Shaw through his essay *The Quintessence of Ibsenism* and through the translations of William Archer. The plays stunned audiences throughout Europe by their honesty and exposure of the hypocrisies of the late 19th century; and were received in similar fashion in the USA, where America's best known 20th century playwright, Arthur Miller, was later to make adaptations of them.

NOTE: It is important to understand that there was much more to Ibsen's plays than simply the use of realistic language.

In addition to Ibsen there were other major influential figures at work such as the Swedish playwright August Strindberg and playwright and master of the short story, Anton Chekhov in Russia.

Whereas Strindberg's plays *The Father* and *Miss*

Julie brought him to the forefront as the exponent of naturalistic drama, Chekhov's early full-length plays had been failures. However, he was finally to achieve success with a revival of *The Seagull* in 1898 at the Moscow Art Theatre and then went on to write his masterpieces *Uncle Vanya, The Three Sisters and The Cherry Orchard.*

NOTE: Both Strindberg and Chekhov continued to develop a sense of 'psychological realism' in all their plays.

In the British theatre we might also identify the work of the 19th century playwright T W Robertson and the actor/manager Sir Henry Irving (1838-1905) as key figures in the development of realism.

Robertson was so concerned with accurate detail in the presentation of his plays that his precise stage directions earned him the nickname 'doorknobs Robertson'.

Irving's 1871 production of Leopold Lewis's obscure play *The Bells* used accurate sound effects and carefully observed, psychologically truthful acting so effectively that the event is sometimes labelled 'the birth of realism' in the British theatre.

19th century realistic plays were usually written in the form known as 'the well-made play' - a play in three or four acts, each with a number of scenes. The overall shape of such a play includes an initial phase of exposition, in which we come to understand the context of the action and the situation of the characters, followed by a series of complications and climaxes.

This form of writing, using 'the well-made play' formula, was popularised by the 19th century French dramatist Eugène Scribe (1791-1861), and remained very popular until the 1950s and 60s.

1950s and 60s social realism

Once again realistic plays were to revolutionise the English-speaking theatre through 'social realism' in the 1950s and 60s.

Plays of this genre include: *Look Back in Anger* - which established the leading exponent of British social drama, John Osborne as the first of the 'Angry Young Men', *Roots* by Arnold Wesker, Shelagh Delaney's first and best known play *A Taste of Honey*, *The One Day of the Year* by Australian playwright Alan Seymour and *Blood Knot* by the South African, Athol Fugard.

All these works presented the speech and living conditions of people living in comparative poverty and in very different social classes from those previously represented in drama on stage.

The ironic description 'kitchen sink' given to British post war plays of this type which used working-class, drab, domestic settings rather than the drawing-rooms of the middle-class, suggested unease with some of their unrelieved realism.

Inevitably there is an element of contrivance in realistic plays. The 'ordinary' language and events portrayed in plays of this genre are actually carefully crafted and the playwright has been highly selective.

Episodic Realism

More recent realistic plays, such as *Teen Dreams* by the British playwright David Edgar, with its scenes in school cloakrooms and classrooms, tend to be written in a series of short scenes - a more **'episodic'** structure.

episodic   having a series of events complete in itself but forming part of a larger one

In all plays of this type it is important to see that the playwright has obviously chosen and shaped very carefully what the audience is to see and hear.

19th Century Naturalism

A more extreme form of realism which attempted to avoid this degree of artificiality was the 19th century artistic movement known as **Naturalism**, of which the French novelist, Emil Zola (1840-1902) was the leading exponent. After his first major novel, *Thérèse Raquin,* Zola wrote a series of twenty books described in the subtitle as

> 'the natural and social history of a family under the Second Empire.'

> Les Rougon-Macquart, Emile Zola

Naturalism an artistic movement; the principals and methods of a group of writers who believed that the writer or artist should apply scientific objectivity and precision in the observation and treatment of life without idealizing, imposing value judgments or avoiding what may be regarded as repulsive.

Zola's favourite novel *The Earth,* one of the vast Rougon-Macquart series, was dramatized by Ménessier and directed by Antoine at the Théâtre Antoine, in 1902 and **naturalistic** 'details' employed in the staging of this production included live chickens!

naturalistic   faithful representation of nature, character, etc. realistically and in great detail with avoidance of stylised or conceptual forms

The 19th century followers of Naturalism believed that human actions are largely determined by heredity but that we are also affected by environment. These two elements led to the belief that works of art must be based on a precise observation of nature and, in the case of drama, on an attempt to reproduce the results on stage.

The careful and detailed stage directions in a play text will often reveal a writer strongly influenced by the ideas of naturalism - and we find this particularly in the plays of Chekhov, Shaw and Miller.

The stage directors, André Antoine (1858-1943), director of Odéon from 1906 in France and David Belasco (1859-1951), who experimented with visual effects in America, took naturalism to its ultimate limits.

THINK ABOUT THIS

> Antoine insisted that his actors behave as if there were a 'fourth wall' erected across the proscenium arch which would only be demolished after the dress rehearsal . . . . .
>
> . . . . . and Belasco diverted a local railway track through the rear of his theatre in order to achieve the total realism of a train passing through!

So we can see that the ideas of realism and naturalism are not confined to the dialogue of plays. The use of lighting, scenery and the adoption of a particular production style, all contribute.

We must think about this at a later stage, but it would be useful preparation to read the preface to the play *Miss Julie* written by Strindberg in 1888, as this is something of a manifesto for a new sense of realism in the theatre.

 USEFUL READING

The preface to *Miss Julie.*

A further fascinating debate concerning realism and naturalism appears in the *Messingkauf Dialogues* - an imaginary dialogue between an actor, a dramaturg and a philosopher written by Bertold Brecht around the late 1930s and early 40s. In one passage there is a lively discussion of the possible failure of both of these 'isms'.

Realism continues to dominate modern writing for the stage, film and television. For example, one of the most successful plays of recent years has been *The Weir* by the young Irish dramatist Conor McPherson. On the surface, at least, this play simply consists of three people sitting in an Irish public house telling stories.

Similarly, American playwright David Mamet's very successful play *Oleanna* shows a series of difficult tutorial meetings between a student and her professor.

Such apparently 'realistic' situations often seem to be a long way from the huge sweep of a Shakespearean drama in which a totally different set of conventions appears to operate.

➩ ASK YOURSELF THE QUESTION

Q Realistic situations have little in common with Shakespearean drama but is it the case?

What is realistic dialogue?

It is misleading to think that realistic dialogue is simply a reproduction of everyday speech.

If we were completely honest we would have to admit that many of our face-to-face or telephone conversations are entirely trivial and often full of private jokes that would be incomprehensible to anyone else.

Added to this, some of us are unable to utter a few phrases without using swear words or other expressions that some listeners might find deeply offensive. So, the total effect on an audience of time spent in the theatre listening to such language would be profoundly boring and alienating.

In the theatre we expect language to have meaning and significance.

Even the most puerile conversations must, of course, have <u>some</u> meaning and significance and the very act of going to the theatre - a specially defined place at a specially defined time, suggests that we are seeking heightened significance and added meaning.

We shall discuss further issues relating to staging in 15 STAGING PLAYS (see p.70), but for the moment we must note that a straightforward transfer to the stage of a string of everyday conversations would make a very inadequate play.

Even simulating the patterns of 'real' conversation is not easy, either. In conversation we rarely speak in complete sentences:

- we pause

- we hesitate

- we repeat ourselves

- we say 'um'

. . . . . and so on.

Perhaps we can begin to see why even a great playwright like Ibsen found the task of writing dialogue that sounded like everyday speech 'difficult'.

In addition to dialogue that sounds like everyday speech we also expect each character to have a distinctive pattern of language, as we all have in real life; and the ability to capture such qualities is the mark of a skilled playwright.

Realistic dialogue, therefore, is actually a clever imitation of reality.

⇨ THINK ABOUT THIS

The first thing I try to do is to make a play live: live as a part of life, and live in its own right as a work of drama. Every character, every life, however minor, to have something to say, comic or serious, and to say it well. Not an easy thing to do . . . . . To me what is called Naturalism or even realism isn't enough. They usually show life at its meanest and commonest, as if life never had time for a dance, a laugh or a song . . . . . so I broke away from realism into the chant of the second act of *The Silver Tassie.*

Sean O'Casey, 1958

Reanimate
Make it
live in its
own right
a work of
drama

II *POETIC DRAMA*

One of the most remarkable features of the drama that originated in Western Civilisation is that many of the most popular and successful play texts have not been written in 'everyday speech' but in verse.

⇨ ASK YOURSELF THE QUESTION:

Q Why is the poetic form of drama so popular?

The reasons for this popularity are very complex and not only should you ask yourself why, you should also discuss this a great deal, too.

poetic written in verse poetry

Clearly, the fact that theatre as we know it has its origins in religious ritual, explains the dramatic use of a heightened sense of language.

It can also be argued that profound levels of meaning and metaphysical issues, when the playwright is seeking to explain the nature of being or reality, are best revealed in poetry. Whereas, more domestic concerns are better handled in prose.

🖙 **Q   WHAT DO YOU THINK?**

Major verse plays in the English language which still have regular performances are mainly drawn from four distinct phases in theatre history: the Classical Greek (see **Ancient Greek plays in translation** p.48), Medieval (see *III MEDIEVAL DRAMA* p.49), Elizabethan and Jacobean (see *IV ELIZABETHAN AND JACOBEAN DRAMA* p.51) and the early 20th Century poetic revival (see *V REVIVING VERSE* p.53).

🖙 TRY THIS: We suggest that you compare this information with 15 STAGING PLAYS (see p.70).

Ancient Greek plays in translation

Now, only a handful of plays remain of the large body of work written for drama festivals in Athens, which were often held in celebration of Dionysus, the god of wine and revelry.

The 7 surviving great tragedies (out of 60 ascribed to him) of Aeschylus - known as 'the father of Greek tragedy', the 7 surviving plays of Sophocles (he wrote 123 plays), the 19 of Euripedes (who wrote about 80 plays), and the 11 surviving comedies of Aristophanes (who is said to have written 54), all date from the 5th century BC.

Although these Classical Greek plays were very popular in their day, to subsequent generations they were only known to a few in university situations where Greek and Latin were far more widely studied and used than they are today.

It was only in the 20th century that English translations of Classical Greek plays were made that were possible to stage.

Invariably, these translations reflected the fact that the originals were written in verse, and play texts revealed a structure of episodes concerned with the **protagonist** punctuated by the words of the Chorus - which may well have sung and danced their commentary on the action in Ancient Greece 2,500 years ago.

protagonist   *the central character in the drama around whom the action centres*

All that we know about the Greek theatre from archaeological sources, art and contemporary writings suggests that a play performance had a strong, ritualistic and non-realistic quality; and the 'rediscovery' of these qualities in early 20th century translations led to some very bold experiments in theatre form and writing.

III   MEDIEVAL DRAMA

In Europe during the Middle Ages and right up until the Reformation a form of drama known as the **mystery play** was developed for performance at Christian festivals.

NOTE: In England, mystery plays were performed at the festival of Corpus Christi, specifically.

mystery plays   *medieval dramatic representations of Biblical events, especially of the life and death of Jesus; they originated in the church liturgy but were later presented by craft guilds in marketplaces*

These plays, which were relatively short would form part of a sequence or 'cycle' of plays which, collectively, told the story of God's creation of the universe and of His subsequent involvement in that creation as described in the *Holy Bible*.

The language of these plays drew substantially on translations of the *Holy Bible* into English of the period, and they were written entirely in verse. Their language is usually simple, direct and poignant and yet the verse forms are often very sophisticated.

All the plays are anonymous and we now simply know them from their town or city of origin. The plays from the northern English city of Wakefield, especially, have very complex rhyme schemes. In all cases, the language makes very effective stage dialogue.

Once again it was the revival of interest in mystery plays and the medieval **morality plays** like *Everyman* in the early years of the 20th century that led to their renewed popularity.

morality plays   *15th and 16th century   allegorical dramas with characters which personify abstractions like Vice and Virtue.*

NOTE: Even more recently 'the Mysteries' have been amongst the most frequently performed and inventively produced plays in the modern theatre.

IV ELIZABETHAN AND JACOBEAN DRAMA

One of the great revolutions in the English-speaking theatre took place when the most significant of Shakespeare's predecessors, the 16th century English playwright, Christopher Marlowe, discovered the strength and variety of blank verse and devised a form of dramatic dialogue based on a ten-syllable line of verse.

Plays such as Marlowe's *The Tragical History of Tamburlaine* and *Dr Faustus*, written in decasyllabic blank verse, excited London audiences by their power, emotional range and ability to deal with great sweeps of history or moments of intense intimacy.

The form was brought to perfection by the great dramatist William Shakespeare, who wrote the most popular, influential and widely performed plays ever created. His use of language included passages of rhyming verse, sometimes in the form of a **sonnet**, passages of **colloquial prose** and sections of **blank verse** so memorable that they have entered into our everyday speech.

> **sonnet** a poem normally of fourteen lines in any of several fixed verse and rhyme schemes characteristically expressing a single theme or idea.

> **colloquial prose** the ordinary form of language with the characteristics of informal commonplace speech.

> **blank verse** unrhymed verse having five iambic metrical feet of two syllables each per line.

Shakespeare's plays appear to be able to encompass every human experience, but perhaps their most remarkable quality is that the verse in which they are generally written provides a text that can be profound, simple or complex, yet credible as 'real dialogue' and superb as a medium for actors.

After Shakespeare, several fine Jacobean English dramatists continued to use verse; and we can see that poetic drama, with its descriptive and image-filled language has an ability to move easily across large tracts of time and space as well as being uninhibited by the need for realism.

However, one of the problems resulting from the success of Marlowe and Shakespeare is that they had many poor imitators who produced nothing more than pale copies of this form of dialogue, displaying an inadequate understanding of the total brilliance of both Marlowe and Shakespeare's work.

⇨ THINK ABOUT THIS

It seems to me that beyond the nameable, classifiable emotions and motives of our conscious life when directed toward action - the part of life which prose drama is wholly adequate to express - there is a fringe of indefinite extent, of feeling which we can only detect, so to speak, out of the corner of the eye . . . . . this peculiar range of sensibility can be expressed by dramatic poetry, at its moments of greatest intensity. At such moments, we touch the border of those feelings which only music can express.

T S Eliot, 1950

V REVIVING VERSE

In the early years of the 20th century the most significant plays being written were those that attempted to simulate the speech of everyday life within a realistic setting.

However, a number of playwrights expressed a growing sense of dissatisfaction with what they saw as the limitations of **prose** drama and attempted to rediscover the power of poetry in the theatre.

prose   the ordinary form of written or spoken language that is not poetry; without rhyme or meter

These playwrights turned largely to the plays of Ancient Greece or to Medieval or Shakespearean drama for their inspiration. In addition, the translations of ancient Japanese *Noh* plays by the poet and critic Ezra Pound (1885–1972) and Ernest Fenelossa provided a further impetus for experimentation.

***Noh**   a classic form of Japanese drama with choral music and dancing using set themes, simple symbolic scenery, elaborately masked and costumed performers and stylised acting*

NOTE: In the same way playwrights in New Zealand, Canada and South Africa have used material drawn from their own rich cultural pasts as a starting point for poetic plays.

Playwrights like the Irish poet and dramatist W B Yeats with his *Plays for Dancers* and the American-born poet and dramatist T S Eliot, whose most successful play was the 1935 *Murder in the Cathedral,* worked, not only to create a poetic language for the theatre, but also to establish new dramatic forms deriving, in part, from ancient and more flexible types of staging.

Productions of this genre had moved away from realism to a less literal view of the function of theatre. The English director William Poel (1852-1934), for example, exerted considerable influence by trying to recreate the physical conditions of the Medieval and Elizabethan theatre with productions such as his 1893 *Measure for Measure* complete with costumed spectators; and Eliot's greatest play had its first performance on a simple stage in Canterbury Cathedral in Kent.

TRY THIS   You might like to pause here and turn to 15 STAGING PLAYS (see p.70).

VI   *EXPRESSIONISM*

The American dramatist Eugene O'Neill turned to writing around 1912 and experimented with many novel theatrical devices and techniques in his quest to express the characters' inner thoughts. He made use of masks in plays such as the 1926 *The Great God*

Brown and employed lengthy 'interior' monologues in his 1928 play *Strange Interlude*.

In O'Neill's 1925 play *The Emperor Jones* we are shown a fictional state ruled over by a dictatorial and self-proclaimed Emperor who is a former criminal. Neither the action nor the dialogue in this play could comfortably be described as realistic and the total effect of seeing this play or even of reading it for the first time is rather like watching a cartoon.

However, there is no doubting the inner reality of the ideas and subject of the play even if the external reality seems distorted. Such a play is described as **expressionist**.

expressionist is a broad term used to describe an artistic approach characterised by a rejection of traditional ideas of beauty or harmony and by the use of distortion, exaggeration, and other non-naturalistic devices in order to emphasise and express the inner world of emotion rather than any external reality.

The term **Expressionism** was introduced into the arts in the very early years of the 20th century by Hervé and the Norwegian painter Edvard Munch (1863-1944), who epitomises the sense of external expression revealing an inner state in his famous picture *The Scream*, an image of fear - the terrifying unreasonable fear we feel in a nightmare.

Expressionism   an early 20th century movement in art, literature and drama characterized by distortion of reality and the use of symbols and stylisation to give objective expression to inner experience

Some critics would argue that the first true Expressionist play was actually *Woyzeck* written by the German playwright Georg Büchner in 1836. This unfinished play is made up of a number of scenes, which are often tiny fragments that can be performed in a number of ways by playing the scenes in different order.

Büchner's *Woyzeck* established the form of plays with terse dialogue, episodic structure and grotesque characterisation which was later developed by fellow German playwright Frank Wedekind, who is best known for his unconventional tragedies in which he anticipated the Theatre of the Absurd, such as the 1891 play *The Awakening of Spring*.

NOTE: Strindberg is more usually credited with writing the first Expressionist play *To Damascus* between 1898 and 1904.

Expressionism in Germany

From about 1910 to 1924, particularly in Germany, Expressionism gave rise to a large body of plays that often required almost dream-like physical settings to enhance their serious and often violent scenes.

NOTE: Such settings could be achieved for the first time by employing the developing techniques of stage lighting and recorded sound.

The language of such plays was expressive, too, and often had soaring, verse-like qualities that sought to express complex ideas and emotions for which ordinary prose seemed inadequate.

Reinhard Johannes Sorge' s 1912 play *The Beggar* is often considered to be the first expressionist play. It shows the struggle between established conventions and new values, between the older and younger generations, and the attempt of a visionary poet to achieve fulfilment in a materialistic and insensitive society.

The influence of Expressionists

The German Expressionists, adopted Strindberg's ideas, developed them, and in turn influenced Irish playwrights such as Yeats and Sean O'Casey and

American playwrights like O'Neill; therefore we can see some of the qualities we have described in their plays, and in much of the contemporary Irish drama, too.

➪ THINK ABOUT THESE

The Expressionist wanted to do more than take photographs. Realising that the artist's environment, as it were, penetrates him and is reflected in the mirror of his soul, he wanted to recreate this environment in its very essence.

Ernst Toller, 1920

The idea for *The Emperor Jones* came from an old circus man I knew.

Eugene O'Neill, 1924

VII EPIC THEATRE

You will have noticed that we have already mentioned the name of Bertold Brecht several times – and the fact is that any serious student of speech and drama is bound to come across the plays, ideas and influences of Brecht before long.

Brecht has been so influential because:

➤ He wrote some of the most memorable plays of the modern age.

➤ He directed the first performances of his plays.

➤ He created a special company, The Berliner Ensemble, to perform his plays.

➤ He developed many distinctive ideas on theatre, directing and acting, which he expressed in a huge variety of books, articles and interviews.

The English-speaking theatre first became aware of Brecht in the mid 1950's and the production of his 1938 play *Mother Courage and her Children* inspired a whole generation of directors, playwrights and actors when it opened in London in 1956.

If you look at the play text of *Mother Courage* you will see that it consists of a series of scenes of very variable length with the events described in the scenes often taking place several months or years apart at various locations in Europe. Some of these scenes contain little more than a cabaret-style song whereas others are complex and full of dialogue and / or action; and sometimes a character will speak directly to the audience. Each scene is introduced with a caption that can either be projected onto a screen or displayed on a placard.

Brecht liked to call this kind of play structure that we have described as Epic Theatre.

For Brecht, theatre going was more like a spectator sport: he never wished to disguise the fact that the stage was simply an arena for action. Lighting equipment was always visible and he made use of music hall and other popular theatre techniques as well as of the latest technical inventions. His plays, like this book, invariably asked the audience the question:

Q WHAT DO YOU THINK?

As a convinced Marxist, Brecht held passionate views on the nature of society and of individual responsibility. His production style rejected the star system and was highly collaborative.

You can see the influences of Brecht at work in almost every aspect of the modern theatre, particularly in the way in which plays are written, and it is well worth following up our suggestions for further reading about Brecht.

SUGGESTED FURTHER READING

Colin Counsell, *Signs of Performance,* Routledge 1996, Chapter 3

Kenneth Pickering, *Studying Modern Drama,* Palgrave Macmillan, 2003, Chapter 7

However, do begin by reading and seeing some of Brecht's plays and then all the other aspects of his work will be more easily understood.

THINK ABOUT THIS

Theatre should have an awareness of the social issues of the time, and in that sense, be a political theatre. A theatre language that working people can understand, but is capable of reflecting, when necessary, ideas, either simple or involved, in a poetic form. An expressive and flexible form of movement, and a high standard of skill and technique in acting. A high level of technical expertise capable of integrating sound and light into the production.

Joan Littlewood, 1956

NOTE: Joan Littlewood directed the first British production of *Mother Courage* in Barnstaple in 1955, in which she played the title role. She pioneered work in left wing, popular theatre and is recognised as one of Britain's most influential theatre directors. Her production style has always drawn heavily on Brechtian and music hall conventions, and this is perhaps best exemplified in *Oh! What a Lovely War,* the 1963 biting satire on the First World War, which she co-wrote with Charles Chilton and directed.

VIII THEATRE OF THE ABSURD

So far we have thought about a number of different kinds of play text and, although our impressions of these plays may vary enormously, there is a degree to which we expect them to 'make sense' when we read them.

However, there are some plays that seem to have no 'meaning' either in terms of what is said or what is done.

Perhaps the most famous play of this kind is Samuel Beckett's 1953 play *Waiting for Godot* in which two characters on a stage bare, except for a tree (which is leafless at the beginning of the play and leafy for the second half), converse in clichés, repetitive patterns and utterances that seem to bear no relation to those made before or after. The two characters, Vladimir and Estragon, give no clues as to their past, their present intentions or future aspirations.

Later, Vladimir and Estragon are joined by two characters in a strange slave / master relationship. One of these, Lucky, makes one of the longest speeches in the modern theatre - a speech which seems totally nonsensical at first reading.

Nothing about the play ever resolves in the way we would expect. There is no real plot; nothing seems to happen and the characters inhabit a universe that appears hostile, threatening and inexplicable. Language is used to fill time and silence, to threaten and to avoid communication.

With so many of our expectations of a play cheated it is remarkable that the play remains one of the most memorable and influential theatrical experiences of all time.

In the 1950s and 1960s, particularly, a number of plays by playwrights such as Beckett, Pinter, David Campton and Ionesco all employed situations and language devoid of the kind of meaning which realistic plays presumed.

NOTE: The Romanian playwright Eugène Ionesco's

one-act plays *The Chairs* and *Rhinoceros* have come to be seen as typical examples of the Theatre of the Absurd.

Ironically, many theatregoers and critics have found the absence of content in the communication of the language and apparent absurdity of the action or inaction of such plays to be much closer to the reality of life than might be expected.

The Theatre of the Absurd produced some telling and disturbing images for life in the modern world and plays from that genre labelled Comedies of Menace create stage metaphors for a world in which people appear threatened by indefinable, external forces.

NOTE: The label 'Comedies of Menace' was a deliberate distortion of **Comedy of Manners.**

Comedy of Manners a type of 17th and 18th century comedy depicting and satirizing the manners and customs of fashionable society

Plays of the Absurd pushed the boundaries of experimentation in all directions and reading a play text you may well find yourself confronted with a play which only lasts a few seconds, a play constantly punctuated by silence or a play in which chairs, headless leaders or dustbins inhabited by the characters are major features!

⇨ THINK ABOUT THIS

> I have often chosen to write plays about nothing, rather than about secondary problems (social, political, sexual, etc.). There is no action in *The Bald Soprano*, simply theatrical machinery functioning, as it were, in a void. It shows a hollow automatism being taken to pieces and put together in the wrong order, as well as automatic men speaking and behaving automatically; and to this extent it illustrates comically the emptiness of a world without metaphysics and a humanity without problems. In *The Chairs* I have tried to deal more directly with the themes that obsess me; with emptiness, with frustration with this world, at once fleeting and crushing, with despair and death.
>
> Eugene Ionesco, 1958

IX PHYSICAL THEATRE

We are going to conclude this brief look at the types of play text we might encounter by considering the increasing popular form of theatre that has little or no written text.

There is always a danger that, because words have traditionally occupied so central a position in plays, we come to consider drama as yet another form of literature, like poetry or the novel.

Although we <u>can</u> read a play and derive something from it as an initial process, it is, of course, the shaping of the text into a physical form that makes it drama.

However, words are not essential for drama.

Many cultures have rich strands of traditional physical theatre that have also influenced the development of English-speaking and Western drama.

In physical theatre it is not the words that predominate, it is the totality of the performance of the actors.

Therefore, many actors are now required to work in demanding situations, using a range of skills and dexterity unknown to many of their predecessors in order to create effective pieces of physical theatre.

Actors may now have to possess acrobatic, juggling and other circus skills, be able to play musical instruments, sing and dance, mime and work with masks or manipulate trick scenery. They may inhabit a performance world of planks or ladders, items that collapse on impact or ropes and swings. They may be surrounded by all manner of sounds and music; and they may use everyday objects in the most unexpected ways

In one such production by a group named *Stretch People*, two actors, using very sophisticated balancing and mime techniques, created a complete scenario of the 'lives' of several upright vacuum cleaners - including the birth of a baby cleaner from the bag of a 'mother'. The entire theatre was held spellbound as one actor, accompanying himself on the guitar, sang a lullaby to the new arrival!

Practitioners of physical theatre have achieved unexpected phenomenal global success with the internationally acclaimed Canadian, *Cirque du Soléil*, which was founded in 1984, the inspiration of a fire-eating street entertainer. The productions feature flawless, highly unusual and visually stunning circus acts without animals, incorporating mime, music and dance, woven around mystic impressionistic story lines. *The Cirque du Soléil* has introduced audiences around the world to a sophisticated spellbinding physical theatre without words.

The development of physical theatre has coincided

with movements from within contemporary dance towards a much more adventurous exploration of the theatrical potential of the human body moving in space. The boundaries of both dance and drama have widened and become less distinct.

NOTE: This is entirely appropriate, for in several Oriental languages you will not find separate words for dance and drama.

⇨ THINK ABOUT THIS

The final destiny of a play is always: to be read. Why shouldn't it begin the way it's going to end anyhow?

Friedrich Hebbel, 1859

15 STAGING PLAYS

Plays really only become drama when we lift them from the page onto the stage.

What is a stage?

➡ ASK YOURSELF THE QUESTION:

Q What is a stage?

This apparently simple question hides a great deal. Many would answer the question by describing the **stage** in a 'traditional' modern Western-influenced theatre.

*(i) **stage** a platform on which plays are presented in a theatre*

Thought of in this way, the 'stage' brings with it images of a raised performing area with an arch in front of it which divides it from an audience, who look on passively from tiered, raked seating. Perhaps it conjures up thick velvet curtains, spotlights, stage scenery and much more!

What you would actually be thinking of if you were to describe a stage like that would be one sort of stage for one type of theatre.

The stage we have described above did not mysteriously come into existence in the long lost past: it is the product of the history of drama and theatre.

In reality, plays do not need a special building or construction to exist. All that plays need is what the famous English theatre and film director, Peter Brook (b.1925), described as 'an empty space': a space that performers and spectators agree will be the place in which the performance takes place.

Theatre is magical. It is magical because it is a product of more than its constituent elements.

to
Quintessence

With consent, a single actor can take an audience to far-off lands, visit dark jungles or stand on the highest mountains. He can do this simply by what he says, the sounds he makes and how he moves or dances. All that is needed is for the audience to allow themselves to be transported into this new world. This is where the idea of a defined **performance area** or stage comes in.

performance area *any area in which actors perform*

➪ LOOK AT THIS EXAMPLE OF BEHAVIOUR

If you were sitting on a train on a bright summer's day

and the man opposite you started to shout -
apparently to himself, about hearing the deafening
sounds of thunder, of feeling the rain lashing his face
and, at the same time, he started to rock almost
uncontrollably from side to side, you might well
believe, and probably quite rightly, that he was unwell.

However, if you were to see exactly the same
behaviour in a place where you know a play is being
performed you would probably start to see him as the
Captain of a ship in a violent storm or as King Lear on
the heath, and not as a sick man.

⇨ ASK YOURSELF THESE TWO QUESTIONS

Q   What is the difference between these two men?

There may well be no difference. The difference is
with <u>you</u>. You have allowed yourself to go on the
journey of theatre; you have allowed yourself to
suspend your disbelief and go with the performer.

Q   Why is that?

There are a number of reasons why you have
suspended your disbelief, but the main reason is one
of space. The most important phrase in this example
of behaviour is:

'A place where you know a play is being performed.'

Because you know it is a performance, you know, through experience, that it is not real. You know that it is signifying something other than the obvious. What is allowing you to make this leap of imagination is the designation of a performance space: in other words, a <u>stage</u>. Without a stage, there can be no drama or theatre.

A stage is, therefore, simply an environment in which both parties, those who are putting on the performance and the spectators, agree that a performance can take place. This agreement or consent allows anything to happen outside the normal logic of everyday life.

A **stage** need not be in a theatre; it need not be a raised platform or, indeed, have any recognisable characteristics other than the fact that it can be defined and agreed upon in some way by both parties. A stage can be a street corner, it can be the top of a double-decker bus or it can even be the bottom of a swimming pool. In fact, a stage can be anywhere, as long as there is mutual consent.

(ii) **stage** *the scene of action*

Stage set design

There is, of course, a second element to the stage, and that is **stage set design**.

stage set design   to design scenery for the stage; scenic design

For once a performance space has been agreed, there is the opportunity to enhance the play visually with the addition of a set and props, as well as costumes and lighting.

It is interesting to look at the varied ways in which Shakespeare's plays have been staged, for example.

Performers

Then there are the **performers**.

performers   those who give a performance by enacting a dramatic role, dancing, singing, etc. before an audience

It is important at this point, to remind ourselves that a play **performance** is not simply about animating a written text that is part of the literary tradition.

performance   a presentation before an audience by a performer

Theatre performances and plays must be thought of equally as visual art. We go to <u>see</u> a play and <u>watch</u> a performance.

So, theatre and drama are truly interdisciplinary: and they can take advantage of almost all the other art forms such as painting, sculpture, song, dance, poetry and narrative prose, etcetera.

All this reminds us that we must think carefully about how our own performances look and sound!

➪ THINK ABOUT THESE

> (Adolfe) Appia conceived of the stage in relation to the action.
>
> Jacques Copeau, 1935

> Let good actors today play in a barn or on a theatre, tomorrow at an inn or inside a church, or in the Devil's name, even on an expressionistic stage: if the place corresponds with the play something wonderful will be the outcome.
>
> Max Reinhardt, 1924

 NOW LOOK AT THE THEATRE ILLUSTRATIONS

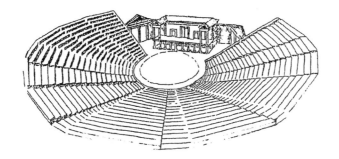

Fig 1   A Classical Greek Theatre

Fig 2   A Medieval Pageant Wagon

Fig 3   *Castle of Perseverance*
A Morality Play in the round

Fig 4   Valenciennes Passion Play 1547

Fig 5   Interior of the Swan Theatre 1596

'Of all the theatres . . . the largest and most magnificent . .
. the Swan; for it accommodates . . . three thousand
persons . . . (roof) supported by wooden columns painted
in such excellent imitation of marble that it is able to
deceive even the most observant . . . its form resembles
that of a Roman work . . .'

Fig 6 *As You Like It* The Norwich Players

Maddermarket Theatre Norwich, the first theatre to be modelled on an Elizabethan indoor playhouse

Fig 7 Richmond Theatre
Restoration Playhouse

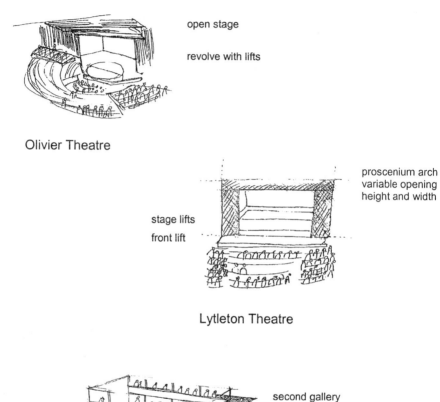

open stage

revolve with lifts

Olivier Theatre

proscenium arch
variable opening
height and width

stage lifts
front lift

Lytleton Theatre

second gallery
first gallery

ground floor space

lidded removable
floor – access to
space below

Cottesloe Theatre

Fig 8   National Theatre   London   England

Three auditoria for performance with front of house spaces
specifically designed for performance plus outdoor galleries
around the buildings

second circular gallery

first circular gallery

Stage space at floor level surrounded by audience on all sides

Fig 9   Royal Exchange Theatre Manchester
         Performance totally in the round with
         galleries stacked in circles above the
         performance space

Fig 10   *Time and the Conways*   J B Priestley
         Produced by Irene Hentschel at the
         Duchess Theatre London 1937

         A traditional box set

Fig 11   *Crest of the Wave*   Ivor Novello
          Theatre Royal   Drury lane *1937*

          The set of Abbey of Gantry Castle
          with ghostly figures

Fig 12   *Richard II*   William Shakespeare
          Peggy Ashcroft and John Gielgud
          Queen's Theatre   London   1937

          Costumes by Motley

Fig 13   *The School for Scandal*   R B Sheridan
Frederick Lloyd, Athene Seyler,
George Howe and Glen Byam Shaw
Queen's Theatre   London 1937

Costumes by Motley

Fig 14   *Amphitryon 38*   Jean Giraudoux
Adapted by S N Behrman
Alfred Lunt
Lyric Theatre London 1938

Classic Greek Costume 1930's style

The study of theatre is NOT the study of a single constantly developing form: there are gaps and breaks.

Throughout history there have been many attempts to create a form of 'stage' and these forms have profoundly influenced the way drama has been performed and thought about. That is why we are now going to look briefly at some of the key points in the history of the stage.

Theatre, plays and performance have probably been with us ever since groups of men and women lived in settled communities. Ritualised performances were probably used to celebrate significant moments within the year such as the gathering of the harvest and the coming of spring.

If there were a kind of theatre of this type it would be realistic to believe that these performances or rituals took place in communal spaces within settlements - in the prehistoric equivalent of the village green or square. We say, 'probably' because there is very little knowledge or evidence of formal theatre prior to the Ancient Greeks.

So it is to the Greeks that we must turn first for some solid information.

X CLASSICAL THEATRE IN GREECE

The first Greek theatre was built in 5th century BC Athens. This theatre, sited on the slopes of the Acropolis, seated some 16,000 spectators and provided the model for all future Greek theatres.

The traditional Greek theatre (see fig 1 p.77) was divided into three sections:

> **the orchestra**, a circular performance or dancing area approximately 20m across.

> **the skene**, initially a temporary and later a permanent structure behind the orchestra from which actors could enter or exit from one of three openings.

> **the theatron**, the auditorium which surrounded half of the orchestra with seating in raised tiered rows.

You will notice at once how these three names for parts of the Greek theatre form the basis for the words orchestra, scene and theatre that are still used today.

Greek plays had a very specific form. Early examples had just one actor supported by a chorus of singers and dancers, and it is widely believed that the whole performance took place more or less in the centre of the orchestra. The orchestra was not raised and there were no barriers between spectators and performers.

In later Greek theatre, the skene started to play a more prominent role and it was raised on a platform with steps leading up to it. This provided a place for the delivery of key speeches and debates.

Early Greek plays were very stylised and written in such a way as not to require specific set design. However, as the plays became more complex with more than one actor, some simple, limited design elements started to appear: a throne, a couch or a painting on the wall of the skene.

We also know that Greek theatrical producers made use of 'special effects'. For example, if a theatre had a permanent stone or wooden skene in place it allowed for the use of a **machina** - a crane-like device used for lowering Gods and other deities into the orchestra.

The **ekkyklema** was one of their more unusual devices: this was a simple trolley used to wheel performers who were often pretending to be dead, out from within the skene to show what had gone on inside!

It would be wrong to think of Greek theatre as stark and bleak because of its comparative lack of stage scenery.

Greek theatre could be truly spectacular.

This was mainly because of the use of increasingly elaborate costumes and the carefully choreographed chorus. The main actors wore built-up shoes to enhance their stature and long, brightly coloured robes and grotesque masks. They also carried props to help the audience recognise characters:

- a king carried a sceptre

- a traveller wore a hat

- the Furies carried flaming torches

Theatrical producers competed with each other to stage the most flamboyant productions but were also very wary of the criticisms made of them if they were seen to overstep the mark and compromise the dignity of the theatre.

Owing to the large scale of Greek theatres the actors' performances had to be big and bold. The excellent acoustics of most theatres allowed certain sensitivity in speech, but the actors were required to use broad and strong gestures in order to communicate across the large distances between them and the furthest member of the audience.

⇨ AN ACTIVITY

Now go back and re-read **Ancient Greek plays in translation** (see 14 TYPES OF PLAY *II POETIC DRAMA* p.48). This will remind you that there have been many recent attempts to use ideas from the Ancient Greek theatre.

Many modern theatre buildings are strongly influenced by what we know of the Greek theatre. The National Theatre, London, was completed in 1976 and the auditorium of the Olivier Theatre with its 'circular' arrangement of raked tiered seating and open-stage, is one such example (see fig 8 p.83).

⇨ TRY THIS

Look for examples of theatre buildings like this – you should be able to find examples for yourself.

⇨ THINK ABOUT THESE

Antique drama was the event, the act itself, not a spectacle.

Adolfe Appia, 1895

You have been over the theatre. Tell me, do you know what is the Art of the Theatre?

Edward Gordon Craig, 1905

XI CLASSICAL THEATRE IN ROME

The theatres of the Roman Empire owed much to the Greeks. Indeed, most, if not all of the Greek theatres were taken over by the Romans and were converted to their needs. So it is probable that there are no unaltered Greek theatres in existence today.

Roman theatres developed in ways that show clear similarities with the theatre buildings we know today.

The **orchestra** was semicircular in a Roman theatre with a much-enlarged **skene** - or stage house. A large platform nearly 2m high, 14m deep and anything from 33m to 100m wide stood in front of this stage house.

The Roman stage house was sometimes as tall as three storeys high and acted as a backdrop. It had five doors with two further doors at either side and was decorated with classical columns, mouldings and statues. Unlike the Greeks before them, the Romans had a very broad taste in the performing arts and these theatres were used for many different types of performances.

NOTE: Many Roman productions lacked the dignity of Greek tragedy or comedy.

It is interesting to see that Roman drama was not particularly influential in the history of theatre - although it did have an impact on later playwrights, such as the Elizabethans in England, who had knowledge of Latin.

XII MEDIEVAL THEATRE

If you turn back to *III MEDIEVAL DRAMA* (see 14 TYPES OF PLAY p.49) you will see that we have described the way in which Mystery Plays and other forms of drama became popular in medieval Europe as part of religious festivals.

The Medieval theatre was NOT a direct descendant of the theatre of classical times; it was more of a reinvention. It is interesting to notice that both the early Greek and Medieval theatre shared the common theme of religious exploration; and when we perform plays from these periods, today, it is important, at the very least, for us to understand how they were originally intended to be staged, to enable us to recapture the spirit of the originals.

Medieval theatre originally centred on the Christian Church and was performed in churches. This was primarily the way in which the *Holy Bible* and the Christian message were communicated to a largely illiterate population.

The faithful were shown scenes from *The Holy Bible* and, as the popularity and scale of these 'productions' grew more than one part of the church was used.

Unlike most of today's theatrical productions, where the audience stays static while the set is changed, in Medieval theatre the audience was required to move to each new scene.

NOTE: By far the most successful recent present-day productions of medieval drama have also used this technique.

By the middle of the 13th century the plays had become more secular in nature and of such a scale that church buildings were no longer suitable. Because of this, the productions moved out of the churches and were taken over by various Trades Guilds, each Guild being responsible for a certain scene or section and its associated 'station'. These outside productions could be of an enormous scale * with over 50 **stations**.

stations   *locations at which the drama took place*

Sometimes these stations were lined up along a street with the audience following as the play progressed.

Sometimes, the stations surrounded a courtyard or square with the audience in the middle, turning appropriately to face the action of a play.

Another solution to providing the audience with a good view of each station was to use wagons (fig 2 p.77). Then the audience was seated or stood in the town square and the wagons processed by, each one presenting a different scene, rather like the floats in a present-day carnival.

Other productions employed yet another solution to the problem of providing the audience with a good view by positioning each of the stations around a common central performance area known as the 'platea', with characters making their entrances through the appropriate stations.

This multi-purpose central performance area, the platea, was to greatly influence the later theatre of Marlowe and Shakespeare.

⇨ THINK ABOUT THESE

> Otto Brahm, on examining Craig's designs for *Venice Preserved* asked 'where is the door'? Craig replied 'there is no door; there is a way in and out!'

> 1910

> A work of art can function only through imagination. Therefore a work of art must constantly arouse the imagination, not just arouse, but activate.

> Vsevolod Myerhold, 1906

XIII ELIZABETHAN THEATRE

Most people would agree that the greatest playwright of all time was William Shakespeare, who was writing plays in England during the reigns of Queen Elizabeth I and King James I.

It is important for us to think about the kind of theatre for which Shakespeare wrote his plays; even though almost every generation since has found ways of staging Shakespeare's plays in accordance with the current fashion.

 FURTHER READING SUGGESTION

Shakespeare the Rewrites by Claire Jones, Dramatic Lines 1999. This is a collection of short female monologue and duologue pieces taken from various fascinating and diverse versions of Shakespeare's plays that provide a glimpse of rewritten plays that take staging and rewriting to interesting limits.

There is a great deal of conjecture as to the exact design of an Elizabethan Theatre because there is little remaining physical evidence. No theatre from that time has remained intact and there are few drawings or plans.

Visitors from abroad at that time were intrigued by the theatres in England and the most famous drawing of an Elizabethan Theatre (see fig 5 p.79) was made by a Dutchman anxious to show his fellow countrymen what he had seen.

There are a number of written descriptions of Elizabethan Theatres but these are usually short and somewhat confusing. However, from what is known we can make a number of assumptions:

➢ An Elizabethan theatre building was circular or square and two or three storeys in height.

➤ An Elizabethan theatre had an open central courtyard with a stage or platform attached to one side with seating or standing room for the audience on all floors on all sides.

➤ The stage was often covered by a roof structure supported by two pillars. This 'heaven' or roof over the stage contained various pieces of apparatus for lifting actors.

In many ways the theatre buildings of the Elizabethan period owed as much to the theatres of Ancient Greece as they did to the more recent staging of dramas of the medieval period. The plays of Shakespeare's time relied little on the idea of the highly elaborate 'station' type of setting and more upon the multipurpose neutral spaces of the orchestra or platea.

LOOK AT 16 A SELECTED HISTORY OF THEATRE: *X CLASSICAL THEATRE IN GREECE* (see p.92) and *XII MEDIEVAL THEATRE* (see p.97) if you need to remind yourself about the meaning of the words 'orchestra' and 'platea'.

Some historians have argued that there may have been some set design feature placed on the back wall of the Elizabethan stage but these could not have formed a vital part of the production because the structure of the theatre would have made it impossible for many people in the audience to see it.

Far more important was the fact that the back wall of the stage contained an entrance on either side and these were clearly used for impressive moments of confrontation, entry of processions and fluid movement across the stage.

The Elizabethans used highly elaborate costumes, like the Greeks before them; and the boy actors who played women wore wigs, magnificent gowns and embroidered gloves. Many actors were skilled swordsmen and they used sharp weapons, and wore helmets and armour, in plays such as *Henry V*.

The Elizabethans were not timid in using the special effects of the day and lowered actors such as fairies in from the 'heavens', for example, and sent up ghosts through the stage trapdoor, as well as using rockets and fireworks.

NOTE: Although various special effects were popular no special lighting was used in Shakespeare's day because plays were performed in daylight. Therefore, an actor carried a candle to let the audience know it was night if a scene required it.

When we read plays by Marlowe and Shakespeare it is possible to recognise the fact that the plays do not require complex stage designs and settings. All the information these playwrights require the audience to know is in the text itself. Everything depended on what the actors did and said and the audience was expected to use its imagination.

Indeed, it could be argued, that the very act of building a complex, realistic set for a play by Marlowe or Shakespeare would almost go against the play itself.

This is also true of Classical Greek theatre: the large open space allowing freedom of movement and freedom of expression exists without the constraints or visual complexity of a 'set'.

This tradition or approach, although coming from the earliest history of the theatre, is very much at the heart of a great deal of modern thinking about the staging of performance.

⇨ THINK ABOUT THIS

To communicate any one of Shakespeare 's plays to a present-day audience, the producer must be prepared to set every resource of modern theatre at the disposal of his text . . . . . in *Romeo and Juliet* the problem was above all to find a modern stagecraft which would give freedom and space to the sweep of the poem. The time for the assumption that *Romeo and Juliet* is a sentimental story to be played against a series of backdrops giving picture postcard views of Italy must surely be gone. It is a play of youth, of freshness, of open air, in which the sky - the great tent of the Mediterranean blue - hangs over every moment of it, from the first brawl in the dusty market to the calm and peaceful cadence of the grave. It is a play of wide spaces in which all scenery and decoration easily become an irrelevance, in which one tree on a bare stage can suggest the loneliness of a place of exile, one wall . . . . . an entire house.

Peter Brook, 1948

But there is, however, another tradition.

XIV THE PICTORIAL TRADITION

Many people still think of a 'stage' as a framed picture and it is certainly true that the majority of plays in the European and English-speaking theatre in the last 350 years have been conceived and produced within what can be described as the 'pictorial tradition'.

This approach to staging plays demands 'realistic', picture-like representations of the places in which the play is set. So, for example, if the action of a play were set in a palace, we would do our utmost to recreate a picture of a palace on stage. As we have already seen in *I REALISM* (see 14 TYPES OF PLAY p.35), this was particularly important for playwrights like Ibsen.

This representational tradition owes something to the extravagant 'stations' of the medieval theatre and to other developments in Renaissance Italy.

In 15th century Italy there was a great rekindling of interest in Classical antiquity, and in particular, architecture and design. This interest was fuelled by the rediscovery of the writing of the Roman architect and military engineer Vitruvius (C27 BC) and it led to the building of a number of new 'classical theatres'.

Also, at this time, the architect Filippo Brunelleschi (1377-1446) invented the system of **linear perspective**. Brunelleschi's discovery in itself was more scientific than artistic, but it became immediately highly important to Early Renaissance artists who developed the practice of 'perspective' painting.

linear perspective   *picturing objects or a scene using converging lines to show them as they appear to the eye with reference to relative distance or depth*

From the 17th century onwards theatre became a matter of 'spectacle' and from being all 'performance' and no real set, it became the opposite: all set and limited performance! The elaborate settings often dwarfed the performers and it was not unusual to see lakes of real water, clouds wafting in the air or real horses racing. Nothing was too much or too extravagant!

At first, these extravagant productions were limited to royal courts but when they moved into the world of independent finance it became difficult to sustain the expense of a special set for each production. So, in this transitional period, reusable design elements appeared.

The inventions included backdrops, flats and stage machinery.

> **backdrops**: perspective was utilised to produce highly 'realistic' backdrops for theatre stages, giving the illusion of three-dimensional space viewed from almost any angle in the theatre.

> **flats:** made of painted canvas on flat wooden frames were used at the sides or 'wings' of the stage.

> **stage machinery:** trapdoors, stage 'flying' systems and trolleys which enabled pieces of the set to be lifted or rolled on and off.

With the new machinery and the creative use of these reusable design features, many different settings could be created without the need for massive reinvestment in each play.

In addition to the financial benefits, all these inventions enabled quicker scene changes to take place, thus satisfying the constant demands for spectacle and realism.

⇨ TRY THIS

Read any play written during this period. If you then think about the play in relation to the pictorial tradition you will understand many of the features of the play and the way in which it is put together.

Theatre today is still indebted to the practices and traditions set up in the 17th and 18th century. Indeed, that flamboyant pictorial tradition dominated European and English-speaking theatre right up until the second half of the 19th century and only began to wane with the demands of playwrights like Chekhov, Ibsen and Strindberg who were exploring a new form of reality.

XV THE REALISTIC TRADITION

Before you read this, go back and read what we have said earlier about realism. (see 14 TYPES OF PLAY I REALISM p.35).

We can now think in a little more detail about some of the implications of this idea for staging plays in a realistic manner.

Realism was, in some respects, another kind of extravagance. Scenery, in the mid to late 19th century, was NOT expressive in the traditional sense but concentrated on the recreation of some type of reality.

Sets were NOT built to <u>suggest</u> a particular place or period - as had the 'stations' in Medieval theatre, but simply to <u>be</u> the place. NO detail was too much. Chairs, tables, stoves and windows were recreated in detail. Producers were obsessed with complete, realistic perfection. Think of 'doorknobs' Robertson!

Theatre of this period was based around the concept of the 'box set' and the 'fourth wall'. The box set was, essentially, the recreation of some kind of imagined or actual room or environment in which the actors were to perform (see fig 10 p.85).

All elements were practical: they actually worked. Characters entered through doors, as opposed to appearing from behind flats in the wings, windows opened and furniture was real. The audience could see into this 'reality' through the fourth and invisible wall in the opening of the proscenium arch.

If you recall Edward Gordon Craig's response to the question about doors posed by Otto Brahm in one of our earlier challenges to ⇨ THINK ABOUT THIS, *III MEDIEVAL DRAMA* (see 14 TYPES OF PLAY p.49) 'there is no door; there is a way in and out!' you will see its significance.

It could be argued that theatre had left the domain of poetry and entered a phase when prose and aspects of realism dominated. The realist theatre did not focus on spectacular events in history or even important events in contemporary life; instead it concentrated on ordinary people and the psychological world in which they existed. So the stage setting had to reflect this shift in focus and producers and playwrights believed that the only way to understand the issues and debates was to show characters in the true setting in which they lived.

Truth only existed in the unadulterated representation of reality and the stage set became a central source of motivation for characters and their psychological development.

This tradition still dominates much of the drama produced today. However, even in its early history, there were those who were uncomfortable with what it implied.

⇨ THINK ABOUT THESE

For a stage set to be original, striking and authentic, it should first be built in accordance with something seen - whether a landscape or an interior. If it is an interior, it should be built with its four sides, its four walls, without worrying about the 4th wall, which will later disappear so as to enable the audience to see what is going on.

Andre Antoine, 1903

The proscenium stage is certainly not out of date.

Tyrone Guthrie, 1959

➡ TRY THIS

Look at the theatre illustrations fig 1 to fig 9, pages 77 - 85. These show a variety of stage forms. Think particularly about the relationship between the actors and the audience in these differing situations.

Whilst the realistic tradition of stage design is still very common in the contemporary theatre, it is by no means the only approach.

We have now moved on from the fussy and elaborate realism suggested by stage director Antoine or playwright Strindberg. Contemporary theatre design is much freer and uses all of the creative opportunities available to us. That is how we should think about the modern stage.

Much of the philosophy and many of the ideas of modern design come from the writing and work of two men who we have already encountered several times who were working at the end of the 19th and beginning of the 20th centuries: Edward Gordon Craig (1872-1966) and Adolphe Appia.

CRAIG

Craig, the English born stage designer, actor, director and theorist was noted more for his theories than for his practical designs, although the designs he left on paper are remarkable.

He settled in Italy in 1908, where he published the theatre journal *The Mask;* which together with his scene designs and his books *The Art of the Theatre* (1911), and *The Theatre Advancing* (1921), had a profound influence on modern theatre practice.

Craig thought of the theatre as an independent art. He criticised the designs of the realist theatre as shabby and foolishly over-reliant on exaggerated, realistic detail. Such designs, he thought, lacked any real artistic vision, purpose or direction, and he believed that great opportunities were being missed.

He believed that only those items essential to the play needed to be seen and that the designer should have as much vision as the director or actor in interpreting the play.

Craig saw great potential in the use of colour and insisted that the designer should strive to create designs that were in harmony with the spirit of the plays through the simple use of symbolic pieces and props.

Craig sought to replace:

- imitation with suggestion

- elaboration with simplicity

APPIA

Adolphe Appia (1862-1928) Scene designer and theatrical producer, was born in Geneva, Switzerland. He was one of the first to introduce simple planes instead of rich stage settings, and he pioneered the symbolic use of lighting.

Appia shared many of Craig's concerns regarding the designs of the realist theatre but, in many ways, was even more revolutionary.

Appia believed:

- the actor was the primary focus of the play

- any design should be in harmony with the living performer

He was less concerned with recreating the actual environment in which a play's character might be, than with trying to explore the 'feeling' that the character would experience of being in that environment or position.

Like Craig, he insisted that the designer, like you, should think about the play. The focus was on the actor. So, for example, if a character were in a busy street, the designer should focus on the ideas of claustrophobia, confusion and noise and NOT on shops, people and cars.

Appia felt that the audience should not be distracted by extraneous detail and activity but should be free to concentrate on the individual performance. The human body was enough of reality without the need for any other kind. In fact, he felt that the setting should put the performers into 'relief' and pull the play along its psychological path by being a visual counterpoint to the structure and spirit of the performance.

To achieve this, Appia created sets on multiple levels, using large, abstract constructions of pillars, cubes, ramps and stairways.

Stage sets within the tradition of Appia were and are characterised by:

- rejection of the realist tradition

- a recognition of the actor as the primary force

- an acceptance and embracing of new technology – particularly lighting

- a stark and uncluttered environment

- multiple stage levels

- the stage setting a tool of action

Clearly, then, for Appia and Craig, the designer was no longer a simple stage decorator but a vital part of the whole creative team.

Decisions about staging had now become a central issue in thinking about plays.

➪ ASK YOURSELF THIS QUESTION

Q   What have you learnt from this very short and very selective look at the history of staging?

We hope this snapshot has illustrated that:

➢   Theatre is as much a visual art as a literary art. Words alone do not make a play.

➢   A play is profoundly affected by the kind of theatre for which it is written.

> Designing for plays is not a secondary activity: it is as important as any other element of theatre.

> The box set and the realist tradition only represent one potential solution to stage design.

THINK ABOUT THIS

The theatre is still largely rooted in the nineteenth century, with its tradition of an entertainment presented on a stage, framed by a <u>proscenium arch</u>, before serried ranks of people. Periodically designers and directors have tried to break with this convention but are thwarted by the archaic convention of <u>flies</u> and other limitations of outmoded buildings . . . . . Indeed, whenever an attempt is made to break through architecturally, it is always, significantly, backwards in time to the <u>apron stage</u> of the Elizabethan playhouse or the Greek arena . . . . . where is the NEW theatre of 2001? For such a theatre what is required is a space which will provide the greatest physical and scenic flexibility, involving <u>grids</u>, <u>hydraulic lifts</u>, <u>revolves</u>, <u>tracks</u>, <u>scrims</u>, <u>screens</u>, <u>domes</u>, <u>levels</u> . . . . . and all able to be lit from above, beneath and every side. The theatre must give the audience of today a new experience of space . . . . . its intimacy and immensity.

James Roose-Evans, 1970

➡ TRY THESE EXERCISES

To help you explore some of the issues we have raised you might like to try the following exercises:

1   Obtain a good dictionary of theatre or staging reference book and look up all the <u>technical terms</u> used in the Roose-Evans extract.

2   Think of a play you have seen performed or were involved in and answer these questions:

   i   Why do you think the designer and director chose to use that particular set and form of staging ?

   ii   How did the set enhance the progress of the play?

   iii What other staging opportunities were available?

   iv   How did the actors relate to the set?

3 Choose a play, or an extract from a play (it may be one you are preparing for an examination) and answer the following questions:

i   What sort of staging do you think the playwright had in mind for the play?

ii What sort of set do you think would be best suited to the play?

iii How would a different style of setting change the performance of the actors or my own performance in the play?

It is possible that you might find this topic a little more difficult to digest than anything that has gone before . . . . but do not give up, it is well worth taking time to read this brief consideration of critical theory.

You can be comforted by the fact that the great, contemporary playwright, Harold Pinter once said that he had never found theory of any use!

We believe that looking at theory can help students to understand, but we must emphasise that we are NOT asking you to learn or remember facts; we are simply suggesting some ways of thinking about plays.

Non-verbal communication

We have already looked at the importance of lighting when it is used as a tool of non-verbal information in 11 LAYERS OF MEANING (see **Non-verbal information** p.27), and we are aware that this applies equally to stage sets, properties, costumes, actions, dances, music, sound as well as special effects (see figs 11 – 14 p.87 and 89).

Now think back to what you have read about Appia. He thought of stage setting as 'a tool of action' and believed that the design should be in harmony with the primary focus of the play - the actor. So he created a stark and uncluttered environment with multiple stage levels for actors and explored the 'feelings' that the characters would experience being in that environment. Appia embraced new technology and had a particular interest in lighting (see 17 DESIGN AND THE MODERN STAGE p.112).

Stage lighting frequently provides us with interesting examples of non-verbal communication such as the brilliant and imaginative staging and lighting designs of American designer Norman Bel Geddes (1893-1958), a visionary not unlike Appia, who is best remembered for his productions of Dante's *The Divine Comedy*, 1921 and his 1931 *Hamlet*.

In the theatre, it is obvious that costume does not communicate in the same way as speech but the spectator certainly interprets it or attaches meaning to it. As we have seen, theatre costume is another 'sign system' by means of which meanings can be constructed and these may 'denote', that is, 'state explicitly' or 'connote', that is, suggest by means of association.

THINK ABOUT THESE

The Norwich Players, an influential English amateur group led by Walter Nugent Monck (1878 -1958) produced *As You Like It* at the Maddermarket Theatre, Norfolk in 1921 with the cast dressed in traditional costumes.

Julie Taymor (b.1952) designed the spectacular costumes and masks for *The Lion King* on Broadway and London's West End as well as directing both productions. Her accomplished aim was to take the epic Disney film, find its essence and make it theatre.

When Peter Brook (b.1925) directed the 1970 production of *A Midsummer Night's Dream* he sought to strip the play of its romantic fairies and woodlands and make it more immediately relevant to his time by costuming the performers in overalls with a few additional *commedia dell'arte* and circus costumes. Brook followed the theme through with actions and sets too - flying was accomplished with trapezes and the forest was loosely coiled metal springs attached to fishing rods.

⇨ TRY THIS

Think of the various ways in which non-verbal communication has been used effectively in productions and find interesting examples.

As we read the text of a play, we are able to make sense of it as a piece of theatre and visualise the action, setting and atmosphere of the play and even discuss the symbolism with the help of these codes and sign systems.

In using terms like 'codes of communication' and 'sign systems' we are borrowing expressions from the type or 'school' of criticism known as **Structuralism.**

Structuralism *structural principals, as in the analysis, organising or application of concepts*

Structuralism has had a profound effect on innumerable aspects of culture in the 20th century.

When it is applied to literature, this method has demolished the traditional idea that the text could function like a transparent screen between the writer and the reader. Previously, it had been assumed that the identity of both the reader and writer and the meaning of the story, had been fixed, and was in some sense 'there', waiting to be discovered.

You may well approach thinking about a play as a structuralist. However, you need to be aware that critics of the Structuralist movement have shown that it is not quite as simple as this, and that the identities of both the reader and the writer are constructed by and through the process of the exchange of communication. You can see that, if **meaning** in literature is constructed rather than found, then the theatre is even more complex, since meaning is constructed both by performers and spectators.

meaning   *what is understood*

The traditional view, which was that the text alone could be reliably preserved, has been called into question. Perhaps the process of reading a text is no more reliable than the process of 'reading' - that is, constructing a meaning for a performance.

You are probably wondering if a new approach such as this is helpful at all! It is, because this approach to literary criticism reminds us that any thinking about theatre must somehow take account of the variety of sign systems through which theatre communicates.

But I don't need any of this! I know a good performance when I see one!

I know a good performance when I see one!

When we go to a live performance we all recognise what we believe to be 'good' theatre or 'bad' theatre. We all know, or rather, feel whether a performance is engaging or tiresome.

➥ ASK YOURSELF THIS QUESTION

Q What is the point of critical theory?

The answer is NOT so that we can reject or forget our emotional responses to a performance but rather that we can start to <u>understand</u> our responses and how performances create them.

Critical theory is NOT about telling us what is 'good' or 'bad' but about <u>how</u> theatre operates so that we can be empowered to make more valuable judgements, whether it is our own involvement in performances as creators - playwrights, producers, actors, set and lighting designers, or as spectators, and readers of play texts for study or pleasure.

critical theory   *careful analysis and judgment of the principals and methods rather than the practice*

There are many approaches to the study of theatre and performance.

NOTE: As with the earlier topics when we looked at the various types of play we must remind you that this brief look at the different ways in which plays may be thought about is NOT a series of 'isms' to be learned!

Arnold and Leavis

A criticism of a play using the method of criticism known as the Leavisite method would not concern itself with how it worked in the theatre but whether its content was of moral worth.

This is the approach to the study of theatre with which you are probably most familiar and it concerns itself almost exclusively with the dramatic text. So the enquiry is not into the performance but rather into the written play and its supposed intended meaning.

In this system of analysis, individual 'characters' within the play are dissected, narrative structures dismantled and plot motivations debated and judged against some idea of moral law.

This approach asks us to look for what we think the playwright intended and rather assumes that there is only one intended meaning dictated by the playwright, who has an almost god-like position of deciding how we should respond of react.

The audience has a very limited role as a passive receptacle of meaning using this system associated with the 19th century British poet and critic, Matthew Arnold (1822–1888), and more recently with the influential British literary critic F R Leavis (1895–1978).

ARNOLD

For Arnold, culture, of which drama is a part, is a fight to save things that are worthy of keeping.

TRY THIS:

You might like to debate the idea that plays of moral worth are the only plays of worth.

LEAVIS

Leavis also stressed the moral value of works and he and his followers believed in a literary 'hierarchy'. So, for them, opera and Classical plays were 'great works', because they demonstrated high moral or cultural value and were part of 'High Art', whereas music hall, popular music or cartoons were looked upon as 'Low Art'.

⇨ TRY THIS:

You might like to draw up 3 columns: HIGH ART * LOW ART * DON'T KNOW. Then, working from the list of suggested plays in PLAYS TO THINK ABOUT (see p.137) select and categorise a cross section of 18 or more.

It's very easy to rubbish this moralistic tradition of criticism which dominated from the 1930's until quite recently, but it did, at least, encourage thinking and it paved the way for some other very interesting approaches which we shall briefly consider now.

Culturalism and cultural studies

⇨ THINK ABOUT THIS

The Culturalist approach insists that by analysing the culture of a society - the textual forms and the documented practices of culture – it is possible to reconstitute the patterned behaviour and ideas shared by the men and women who produce and consume the culture texts of that society.

Storey, 1993

In this short quotation, the writer has summed up a new approach to thinking about the arts, which became known as **Culturalism**. It is really what you are doing when you are answering a question about the conditions and attitudes of a society which created a play.

Culturalism   *looking at the ideas, customs, etc. of a given people in a given period*

HALL, HOGGART AND WILLIAMS

Three names, Stuart Hall, Richard Hoggart and the Welsh social historian and critic Raymond Williams (1921–1988) are associated particularly with this rejection of the Leavisite method of criticism.

For thinkers like Hall, Hoggart and Williams, the study of a play text was not about evaluating it against some already existing set of values but about discovering and understanding the society that produced and consumed it.

They placed the spectator or audience in a more central position because they argued that it is the audience who actually create the meaning of the text.

NOTE: In order to do this, of course, the audience use their own cultural experience.

Ideology

The concept that is central to what we might call cultural studies discourse, is ideology. There are many definitions of ideology but it is useful to think about some of them, particularly those linked to the writings of the German founder of international communism, Karl Marx (1818 -1883), as these form the basis of much recent critical theory.

If they were asked to define ideology, most people would respond by saying something like 'an ideology is simply a grouping of ideas or beliefs'. This is a politically neutral concept and is NOT of much use to us as a tool for a theatre or cultural critic.

However, for the Classical Marxist, ideology is far from being neutral or passive, but a highly political concept concerned with the whole issue of power and control. For Marxists, ideology is about distortion, concealment and masking of reality; it is about the construction and maintenance of power so as to perpetuate the dominance of one group over another.

⇨ ASK YOURSELF THE QUESTION

Q   Why do we need to concern ourselves with the concept of ideology when thinking about theatre?

For a Marxist critic, all cultural texts, such as plays, are political, offering partial images of the world.

If, then, you are to study theatre, and, among other things, think about them from a Marxist point of view, the concept of ideology is essential in the search for meaning. Theatre and drama, like all cultural texts, are for the Marxist, the battle ground for the class struggle and the site of power and potential control.

NOTE: We must make it clear that YOU DO NOT HAVE TO BE A MARXIST to be able to benefit from this way of thinking.

However, it is quite possible that you might learn about modern theatre, for example, from a book by the Welsh Social historian, critic and professor of drama, Raymond Williams (1921-1988) who was active in New Left intellectual movements, and be able to detect his standpoint.

 SUGGESTED READING

> *Drama from Ibsen to Brecht,* by Raymond Williams

DON'T forget, that the moment you think about a play, you are, to some extent, a 'cultural critic'.

We have already pointed out our use of the word **'code'** as a way of making sense of theatre, now we shall meet the word again.

The other word you need to get used to seeing is **'discourse'**, which is a communication of ideas, an exchange of ideas; a conversation.

An important article by Stuart Hall (b.1942) entitled *'Encoding and Decoding in the Television Discourse'* appeared in the *British Culture Studies* journal in 1973, in which he put forward a way of looking at performance using a version of the Marxist notion of ideology.

It is worth looking at the diagram Hall produced, bearing in mind that the 'discourse' is the process that is going on when a spectator interacts with a performance of some kind. This diagram works for any live performance and we can see that the 'discourse' passes through three distinct phases.

NOTE: Once again, do not be frightened by the way these ideas are conveyed, this is only another way of thinking about plays.

Stuart Hall Model of Encoding-Decoding - Hall 1973

amended for theatrical performance

Programme as
Meaningful Discourse

(Theatrical Performance 1*)

Encoding   Decoding

Meaning   Meaning

Structure 1   Structure 1

Frameworks of Knowledge   Frameworks of Knowledge

- - - - - - - - - -   - - - - - - - - - -

Relations of Production   Relations of Production

- - - - - - - - - -   - - - - - - - - - -

Technical Infrastructure   Technical Infrastructure

➡ NOW THINK ABOUT THESE 3 PHRASES:

I Encoding Meaning

Firstly the theatre professional (actor, director, designer, etc.) translates the raw dramatic text into a theatrical performance. To do this, he or she will be using all their technical skill, knowledge of production conventions and performance experience. These are all 'ideological constructions' because they will all be based on a specific concept or notion of what theatre is and what it is for.

So when we explore this phase we should ask ourselves several questions.

Q Why is the performance being staged?

Q Who gains what 'profit' from the performance?

Q Who is the performance for?

We can gain a great deal from such questions.

For example, a Broadway musical will make us very aware that the production is a very commercial enterprise; the producer will want to ensure that everyone wants to go to see it and will avoid anything too offensive or obscure. Therefore the production will probably rely on a clear-cut story line and familiar performance techniques, together with a 'star' in the lead role.

On the other hand, if we know that a performance is being produced by a theatre company with 'left wing' political affiliations, made up of non-professional performers, staged in a trades union or church hall, we can make certain assumptions about the ideological forces in the play. We can assume that the production is not designed simply to entertain but that there are distinct 'messages' and positions in the play, and some of the conventions of mainstream theatre will be rejected or subverted.

2 Programme as Meaningful Discourse

Secondly, once constructed and in performance, the message or meaning of the play is no longer tied to a single idea but is now open to re-reading. This is what you do whenever you watch a play.

3 Decoding

Thirdly, the audience 'decodes' the theatrical discourse. Here, the same ideological pressures come into play and there is no guarantee that there will be any consistency in meaning. The audience brings its own cultural and other issues so that, for example, a Western, European audience watching a Kathakali dance from Southern India would not 'read' or 'decode' the performance in the same way as an Indian audience well versed in the highly stylised and coded performance.

As we have seen, individual spectators from broadly the same society may read the texts in any number of different ways depending on their own ideological, cultural or political positions. They may accept the encoding systems of the producers and decode the performance in a manner that recreates the producer's preferred meaning. However, they may also, of course, take the opposite approach and produce a reading totally in opposition to the producer's intention. Most likely, the audience will enter into a 'negotiated meaning', by which we mean that that certain elements may be agreed and others rejected.

At the heart of the diagram by Hall and much of the critical thinking since the 1960's, is the idea of 'signs'. The various new approaches to criticism we have outlined remind us that, whenever we think about plays in performance, we must somehow take account of the variety of 'sign systems' through which the theatre communicates.

This takes us back to the Structuralists because it was they, especially the French writer and critic Roland Barthes (1915 – 1980), who addressed the analysis of the text as a system of signs whose underlying structure forms the meaning of the work as a whole. Barthes developed the idea of the sign system to show that we are perpetually 'reading' messages in the objects that surround us . . . . . but these are not spoken messages . . . . . messages such as these are not conveyed in words.

Almost everything around us, from traffic lights to the latest dress fashion, conveys meaning to us, and offers a set of coded signs for us to interpret, both consciously and sometimes subconsciously. You might like to refer back to **non-verbal communication**. (see 18 CRITICAL THINKING ABOUT PLAYS p.120).

Some of what we have been saying in the last few pages may seem a very long way from useful preparation for a performance or drama examination but it is important that you have been introduced to some of the thinking that has been going on in the world that is now often described as Theatre and Performance Studies. Every college or university where drama is studied now has to take note of all the most recent thinking about plays and the way we look at them.

We hope that you now realise that every decision you take and every comment you make needs careful thought.

If any of the ways of thinking about plays we have introduced seem to be of no use, reject them!

On the other hand, if you now realise that there are many other possible ways of thinking about plays that are new to you . . . . . whether you are writing plays, directing, acting or designing for the stage, watching plays or reading play texts, writing about plays or simply discussing them . . . . . GOOD.

Here is a list of all the playwrights we have mentioned, together with suggestions for plays you might like to read and think about.

Aeschylus (c.525 - c.456 BC) *Agamemnon.*

Aristiphanes (c.448 - c.388 BC) *The Wasps; Peace; Lysistrata: The Plutus.*

Alan Ayckbourn (b.1939) *Relatively Speaking; The Norman Conquests.*

Samuel Beckett (1906 - 1989) *Krapp's Last Tape; Breath: Waiting for Godot; Happy Days: Endgame.*

Bertolt Brecht (1898 - 1956) *Mother Courage and her Children; The Good Person of Setzuan; The Threepenny Opera; The Caucasian Chalk Circle.*

Georg Büchner (1813 - 1837) *Woyzek; The Death of Danton.*

David Campton (b.1924) *At Sea; Four Minute Warning.*

Anton Chekhov (1860 - 1904) *The Seagull; Uncle Vanya; The Three Sisters; The Cherry Orchard.*

Shelagh Delaney (b.1939) *A Taste of Honey.*

David Edgar (b.1948) *Teen Dreams; The National Interest: Mary Barnes.*

T S Eliot (1888 - 1965) *Murder in the Cathedral; The Family Reunion; The Cocktail Party.*

Kevin Elyot (b.1951) *My Night With Reg; Coming Clean.*

Euripedes (c. 480 - 406 BC) *Alcestis; The Bacchae.*

Athol Fugard (b.l932) *Blood Knot; My Children, my Africa.*

David Hare (b.1947) *Via Dolorosa; Fanshen.*

Václev Havel (b.1936) *Sorry; The Garden Party, The Conspirators.*

Henrik Ibsen (1828 - 1906) *Ghosts; A Doll's House; The Wild Duck.*

Eugène Ionesco (1912 - 1994) *The Bald Soprano; The Chairs; Rhinoceros.*

Ann Jellicoe (b.1927) *The Knack; The Sport of my Mad Mother.*

Ben Jonson (1572 -1637) *Every Man in His Humour; Volpone; The Alchemist.*

Mike Leigh (b.1943) *Abigail's Party; Nuts in May* [television plays].

Leopold Lewis (1840 - 1891) *The Bells.*

Joan Littlewood (b.1914) & **Charles Chilton** *Oh! What a Lovely War.*

Greg Magee (b.1950) *Foreskins' Lament.*

David Mamet (b.1947) *Oleanna; American Buffalo; Speed the Plough.*

Chrlstopher Marlowe (1564 - 1593) *The Tragical History of Tamburlaine the Great; Dr Faustus.*

Bruce Mason (1921 - 1982) *The End of the Golden Weather.*

Conor Mc Pherson (b.1971) *The Weir.*

Arthur Miller (b.1916) *Death of a Salesman; The Crucible.*

Sean O'Casey (1880 - 1964) *The Silver Tassie; Juno and the Paycock; The Plough and the Stars.*

Eugene O'Neill (1888 - 1953) *The Emperor Jones; The Great God Brown; Strange Interlude; Long Day's Journey into Night.*

John Osborne (1929 - 1994) *Look Back in Anger; The Entertainer; Luther.*

Harold Pinter (b.1930) *The Caretaker; The Birthday Party.*

J B Priestley (1894 - 1984) *An Inspector Calls; Dangerous Corner; Time and the Conways.*

Lynn Riggs (1899 -1954) *Green Grow the Lilacs*

T W Robertson (1829 - 1871) *Caste.*

Eugène Scribe (1791 - 1861) *Marriage for Money; A Glass of Water; Adrienne Lecouvreur.*

Alan Seymour (b.1927) *The One Day of the Year; A Break in the Music*

William Shakespeare (1564 - 1616) *A Midsummer Night's Dream; Macbeth; Romeo and Juliet; Richard II.*

George Bernard Shaw (1856 - 1950) *Pygmalion; Saint Joan.*

Sophocles (c.496 - 406 BC) *Oedipus Rex.*

Reinhard Johannes Sorge (1892 - 1916) *The Beggar.*

August Strindberg (1849 - 1912) *To Damascus; Ghost Sonata; Miss Julie; The father.*

Shawn Telford (b.1975) *That Kind of Couple.*

Ernst Toller (1893 - 1937) *Masses and Man.*

Frank Wedekind (1864 - 1918) *The Awakening of Spring; Earth Spirit; Pandoras Box; Lulu.*

Arnold Wesker (b.1932) *Chips with Everything; The Kitchen; Roots.*

Thornton Wilder (1897 - 1975) *The Skin of Our Teeth; Our Town; the Matchmaker.*

Tennessee Williams (1911 - 1983) *A Streetcar Named Desire; Cat on a Hot Tin Roof; Night of the Iguana.*

W B Yeats (1865 - 1939) *Plays for Dancers; Cathleen ni Houlihan; At the hawk's Well.*

Emil Zola (1840 - 1902) *The Earth; Jacques Damour* [dramatizations].

ADDITIONAL TITLES

All books may be ordered direct from:

DRAMATIC LINES   PO BOX 201   TWICKENHAM   TW2 5RQ   ENGLAND

freephone: 0800 5429570
tel: 442082969502
fax: 020 8296 9503
e: mail@dramaticlinespublishers.co.uk
www.dramaticlines.co.uk

MONOLOGUES

THE SIEVE
AND OTHER SCENES

Heather Stephens
ISBN 0 9522224 0 X

The Sieve contains unusual short original monologues valid for junior acting examinations. The material in The Sieve has proved popular with winning entries worldwide in drama festival competitions. Although these monologues were originally written for the 8-14 year age range they have been used by adult actors for audition and performance pieces. Each monologue is seen through the eyes of a young person with varied subject matter including tough social issues such as fear, 'Television Spinechiller', senile dementia , 'Seen Through a Glass Darkly' and withdrawal from the world in 'The Sieve'. Other pieces include: 'A Game of Chicken', 'The Present', 'Balloon Race' and a widely used new adaptation of Hans Christian Andersen's 'The Little Match Girl' in monologue form.

CABBAGE
AND OTHER SCENES

Heather Stephens
ISBN 0 9522224 5 0

Following the success of The Sieve, Heather Stephens has written an additional book of monologues with thought provoking and layered subject matter valid for junior acting examinations. The Cabbage monologues were originally written for the 8-14 year age range but have been used by adult actors for audition and performance pieces.   The Aberfan slag heap disaster issues are graphically confronted in   'Aberfan Prophecy' and 'The Surviving Twin' whilst humorous perceptions of life are observed by young people in 'The Tap Dancer' and 'Cabbage'. Other pieces include: 'The Dinner Party Guest', 'Nine Lives' and a new adaptation of Robert Browning's 'The Pied Piper' seen through the eyes of the crippled child.

ALONE IN MY ROOM
ORIGINAL MONOLOGUES

Ken Pickering

ISBN 0 9537770 0 6

This collection of short original monologues includes extracts from the author's longer works in addition to the classics. Provocative issues such as poverty and land abuse are explored in 'One Child at a Time', 'The Young Person Talks' and 'Turtle Island' with adaptations from 'Jane Eyre', Gulliver's Travels' and 'Oliver Twist' and well loved authors include Dostoyevsky. These monologues have a wide variety of applications including syllabus recommendation for various acting examinations. Each monologue has a brief background description and acting notes.

DUOLOGUES

PEARS

Heather Stephens

ISBN 0 9522224 6 9

These thought provoking and unusual short original duologues provide new material for speech and drama festival candidates in the 8-14 year age range. The scenes have also been widely used for junior acting examinations and in a variety of school situations and theatrical applications. Challenging topics in Pears include the emotive issues of child migration, 'Blondie', 'The Outback Institution' and bullying 'Bullies', other scenes examine friendship, 'The Best of Friends', 'The Row' and envy, 'Never the Bridesmaid'. New adaptations of part scenes from cl 'Peace' by Aristophanes and 'Oliver Twist' by Charles Dickens are also included.

TOGETHER NOW
ORIGINAL DUOLOGUES

Ken Pickering

ISBN 0 9537770 1 4

This collection of short duologues includes extracts from Ken Pickering's longer works together with new original pieces. The variety of experiences explored in the scenes can all be easily identified with such as an awkward situation, 'You Tell Her', and the journey of self knowledge in 'Gilgamesh' whilst 'Mobile phones', 'Sales' and 'Food' observe realistic situations in an interesting and perceptive way. Other duologues based on well known stories include 'Snow White' and 'The Pilgrim's Progress'. Each piece has a brief background description and acting notes. The scenes have syllabus recommendation for a number of examination boards and wide variety of theatrical and school applications.

SHAKESPEARE THE REWRITES

Claire Jones
ISBN 0 9522224 8 5

A collection of short monologues and duologues for female players. The scenes are from rewrites of Shakespeare plays from 1670 to the present day written by authors seeking to embellish original texts for performances, to add prequels or sequels or satisfy their own very personal ideas about production. This material is fresh and unusual and will provide exciting new audition and examination material. Comparisons with the original Shakespeare text are fascinating and this book will provide a useful contribution to Theatre Study work from GCSE to beyond 'A' level. Contributors include James Thurber (Macbeth) Arnold Wesker (Merchant of Venice) and Peter Ustinov (Romanoff and Juliet). The collection also includes a most unusual Japanese version of Hamlet.

RESOURCES

DRAMA LESSONS IN ACTION

Antoinette Line
ISBN 0 9522224 2 6

Resource material suitable for classroom and assembly use for teachers of junior and secondary age pupils. Lessons are taught through improvisation. and are not presented as 'model lessons' but provide ideas for adaptation and further development. Lessons include warm-up and speech exercises and many themes are developed through feelings such as timidity, resentfulness, sensitivity and suspicion. Material can be used by groups of varying sizes and pupils are asked to respond to interesting texts from a diverse selection of well known authors including: Roald Dahl, Ogden Nash, Ted Hughes, Michael Rosen, and Oscar Wilde.

AAARGH TO ZIZZ
135 DRAMA GAMES

Graeme Talboys
ISBN 0 9537770 5 7

This valuable resource material has been created by a drama teacher and used mostly in formal drama lessons but also in informal situations such as clubs and parties. The games are extremely flexible, from warm up to cool down, inspiration to conclusion and from deadly serious to purest fun and the wide variety ranges from laughing and rhythm activities to building a sentence and word association. Games such as Do You Like Your Neighbour? could be used as part of a PSHE programme together with many of the activities connected with 'fair play'. The games are easily adapted and each has notes on setting up details of straightforward resources needed. All this material has been used with a wide range of young people in the 10 - 18 year age range.

DRAMA·DANCE·SINGING
TEACHER RESOURCE BOOK

edited by John Nicholas
ISBN 0 9537770 2 2

This collection of drama, dance and singing lesson activities has been drawn from a bank of ideas used by the Stagecoach Theatre Arts Schools teachers. Lessons include speech and drama exercises, games and improvisations often developed as a response to emotions. Dance activities include warm-ups, basic dance positions, improvisations, versatile dance exercises and routines while singing activities help to develop rhythm and notation as well as providing enjoyable games to develop the voice. Activities can be adapted for large or small group use and are suitable for 6 - 16 year olds in a fun yet challenging way.

MUSICAL PLAYS

THREE CHEERS FOR MRS BUTLER   adapted by Vicky Ireland

ISBN 0 9537770 4 9

This versatile musical play about everyday school life is for anyone who has ever been to school. It features the poems and characters created by Allan Ahlberg with a foreword by Michael Rosen, songs by Colin Matthews and Steven Markwick and was first performed at the Polka Theatre for Children, London. The two acts of 40 minutes each can be performed by children, adults or a mixture of both and the play can be produced with a minimum cast of 7 or a large cast of any size.

INTRODUCING OSCAR
The Selfish Giant & The Happy Prince

Veronica Bennetts
ISBN 0 9537770 3 0

Oscar Wilde's timeless stories for children have been chosen for adaptation because of the rich opportunities offered for imaginative exploration and the capacity to vividly illuminate many aspects of the human condition. The original dialogue, lyrics and music by Veronica Bennetts can be adapted and modified according to the needs of the pupils and individual schools or drama groups. The Selfish Giant runs for 25 minutes and The Happy Prince for 1 hour 15 minutes. Both musical can be used for Trinity College, *London.* examinations and are ideal for end of term productions, for drama groups and primary and secondary schools.

A CD backing track for The Selfish Giant & The Happy Prince is available.

TEENAGE PLAYS

WHAT IS THE MATTER WITH MARY JANE?   Wendy Harmer
ISBN 0 9522224 4 2

This monodrama about a recovering anorexic and bulimic takes the audience into the painful reality of a young woman afflicted by eating disorders. The play is based on the personal experience of actress Sancia Robinson and has proved hugely popular in Australia. It is written with warmth and extraordinary honesty and the language, humour and style appeal to current youth culture. A study guide for teachers and students by Dianne Mackenzie, Curriculum Officer for English and Drama, New South Wales is included in this English edition ensuring that the material is ideal for use in the secondary school classroom and for PSHE studies, drama departments in schools and colleges in addition to amateur and professional performance.

X-STACY
Margery Forde
ISBN 0 9522224 9 3

Margery Forde's powerful play centres on the rave culture and illicit teenage drug use and asks tough questions about family, friends and mutual responsibilities. The play has proved hugely successful in Australia and this English edition is published with extensive teachers' notes by Helen Radian, Lecturer of Drama at Queensland University of Technology, to enrich its value for the secondary school classroom, PSHE studies, English and drama departments.

ASSEMBLIES

ASSEMBLIES! ASSEMBLIES! ASSEMBLIES!   Kryssy Hurley
ISBN 0 9537770 6 5

These teacher-led assemblies require minimum preparation and have been written by a practising teacher to involve small or large groups. Each assembly lasts 15-20 minutes and is suitable for Key Stages 2 and 3. There are 12 for each term and these explore many PSHE and Citizenship issues including bullying, racism, friendship, co-operation, feeling positive, making responsible choices and decisions, school rules and laws outside school. All have the following sections: *Resources and Organisation, What to Do, Reflection Time* and *Additional Resources and Activities.* The assemblies are both enjoyable and informative for pupils participating and audiences alike.

SCENES FOR TWO TO TEN PLAYERS

JELLY BEANS   Joseph McNair Stover

ISBN 0 9522224 7 7

The distinctive style and deceptively simple logic of American writer Joseph McNair Stover has universal appeal with scenes that vary in tone from whimsical to serious and focus on young peoples relationships in the contemporary world. The 10 to 15 minute original scenes for 2, 3, and 4 players are suitable for 11 year old students through to adult. Minimal use of sets and props makes Jelly Beans ideal for group acting examinations, classroom drama, assemblies, and a wide variety of additional theatrical applications.

SCENES 4 3 2 10 PLAYERS   Sandy Hill

ISBN 0 9537770 8 1

There are 10 original scenes in the book written for 3 to 10 players with opportunities for doubling-up of characters and introduction of optional additional players. The versatile scenes are of varying playing times and are suitable for performers from as young as 7 through to adult. The flexible use of sets and props have made these pieces particularly useful for group acting examinations and have proved to be immediately popular and successful for candidates as well as winning entries at drama festivals, they can also be used effectively for classroom drama and school assemblies. The scenes are often quirky and vary in tone with unusual endings. They will be enjoyed by performers and audiences alike.

ONE ACT PLAYS

WILL SHAKESPEARE SAVE US!   Paul Nimmo
WILL SHAKESPEARE SAVE THE KING!   ISBN 0 9522224 1 8

Two versatile plays in which famous speeches and scenes from Shakespeare are acted out as part of a comic story about a bored king and his troupe of players. These plays are suitable for the 11-18 year age range and have been produced with varying ages within the same cast and also performed by adults to a young audience. The plays can be produced as a double bill, alternatively each will stand on its own, performed by a minimum cast of 10 without a set, few props and modern dress or large cast, traditional set and costumes. The scripts are ideal for reading aloud by classes or groups and provide an excellent introduction to the works of Shakespeare. Both plays have been successfully performed on tour and at the Shakespeare's Globe in London.

SUGAR ON SUNDAYS
AND OTHER PLAYS

Andrew Gordon
ISBN 0 9522224 3 4

A collection of six one act plays bringing history alive through drama. History is viewed through the eyes of ordinary people and each play is packed with details about everyday life, important events and developments of the period. The plays can be used as classroom drama, for school performances and group acting examinations and can also be used as shared texts for the literacy hour. The plays are suitable for children from Key Stage 2 upwards and are 40-50 minutes in length and explore Ancient Egypt, Ancient Greece, Anglo-Saxon and Viking Times, Victorian Britain and the Second World War. A glossary of key words helps to develop children's historical understanding of National Curriculum History Topics and the plays provide opportunities for children to enjoy role play and performance.

DRAMATIC LINES HANDBOOKS in association with
Trinity, The International Examinations Board

THINKING ABOUT PLAYS
ISBN 1 904557 14 7

Ken Pickering and Giles Auckland-Lewis

☐

SPEECH AND DRAMA
ISBN 1 904557 15 5

Ann Jones and Robert Cheeseman

☐

EFFECTIVE COMMUNICATION
ISBN 1 904557 13 9

John Caputo, Jo Palosaari and Ken Pickering

☐

ACTING SHAKESPEARE FOR AUDITIONS AND EXAMINATIONS
ISBN 1 904557 10 4

Frank Barrie

☐

PREPARING FOR YOUR DIPLOMA IN DRAMA AND SPEECH
ISBN 1 904557 11 2

Kirsty N Findlay and Ken Pickering

☐

MUSICAL THEATRE
ISBN 1 904557 12 0

Gerry Tebbutt